ANDREA L. SHEDLETSKY

Making an Old-Fashioned
PATCHWORK SAMPLER QUILT
on the Sewing Machine

Full-Size Templates and Complete Instructions
for 24 Quilt Blocks

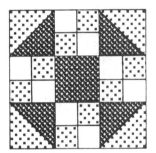

DOVER PUBLICATIONS, INC.
NEW YORK

ACKNOWLEDGMENTS

I made only one of the five quilts photographed in this book—the quilt on the front cover. The other four were made by friends—and are their first efforts at quiltmaking. (A fact that I hope you find very motivating!) The blue and rust quilt on the inside front cover was made by Naomi Brocki. On the inside back cover, the yellow, pink and purple quilt was made by Patricia Cleary and the crayon-colored calico by Mary Brenda Joyner. The peach and green quilt on the back cover was made by Kim Hoffman Daley. I want to thank them for sharing their quilts with me—and with you.

I don't know if every creative person has someone who will hold a hand, give a gentle nudge or help along a dream. I certainly do. To him, thank you.

A.L.S.

Published in Canada by General Publishing Company, Ltd., 30 Lesmill Road, Don Mills, Toronto, Ontario.

Published in the United Kingdom by Constable and Company, Ltd., 10 Orange Street, London WC2H 7EG.

Making an Old-Fashioned Patchwork Sampler Quilt on the Sewing Machine is a new work, first published by Dover Publications, Inc., in 1984.

Edited by Linda Macho
Book design by Barbara Effron

Manufactured in the United States of America
Dover Publications, Inc., 31 East 2nd Street, Mineola, N.Y. 11501

Library of Congress Cataloging in Publication Data

Shedletsky, Andrea L.
    Making an old-fashioned patchwork sampler quilt on the sewing machine.

    (Dover needlework series)
    1. Quilting. 2. Patchwork. 3. Machine sewing. I. Title. II. Series.
TT835.S464 1983   746.9'7'041   83-6224
ISBN 0-486-24588-8

Introduction

My grandmother, a wise and wonderful woman, says that when you cut your own firewood, "it heats you twice." She doesn't pretend that this is an original thought, but it is a true one. Making quilts is a lot like cutting your own firewood: it "warms you twice," and more. Very literally, quilting on a cold winter night will keep you warm. But, making a quilt will warm your heart as well as your feet. From the very beginning, the work is a joy. You use colors and prints that you love; you choose a pattern that you have always liked. As you work, tracing, cutting and sewing, you find that your fabrics are soft and pliable; they feel good in your hands. From bits and pieces that you come to know well, grows a quilt. When it is finished, it is your very own. You don't prop it on your sofa or stash it in your closet—you cuddle under it. You find that it really does warm your feet. And the "oohs" and "aahs" of admiring family and friends warm your heart.

I am inviting you to discover this exciting and heart-warming craft. The quilt in this book is a sampler quilt. It is made up of twenty-four different traditional quilt blocks; see *Diagram 5* on page 14. Some are very easy to sew; others are a bit more difficult. (By the time you get to the "difficult" ones, they won't seem hard at all— just interesting.) Along with full-size templates, and lots of charts and illustrations, I will give you all the advice and help I can.

Quilters can be very opinionated. Generations of quilt-makers saying that you must do something just "this" way can be very convincing. To be sure, every quilter finds his or her own way of doing things. Sometimes, there really is a better or an easier way. But, there are no rules in quiltmaking. If you have been told that the only good quilt is a hand-sewn one, and believed it—forget it. This quilt was designed to be sewn on a machine. So, with that in mind, gather up your supplies, sharpen your pencil, drag out your machine and let's get started!

P.S.: This book is a workbook. It is meant to be cut up, colored in and otherwise used to help you make a wonderful patchwork quilt. By the time you are finished with the book, it may be a bit tattered and worn, but your quilt will be beautiful.

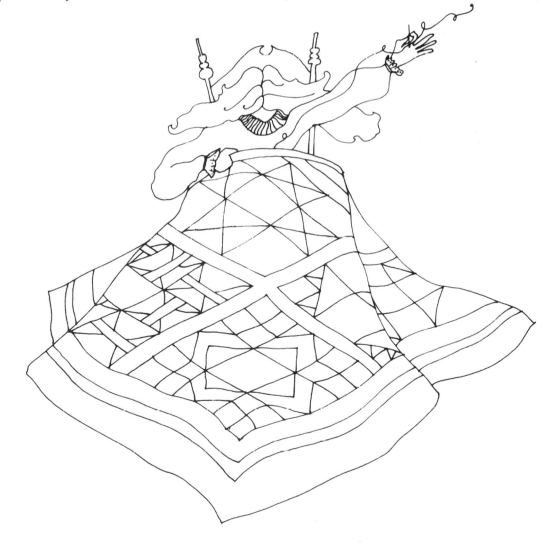

Making an Old-Fashioned Patchwork Sampler Quilt on the Sewing Machine

EQUIPMENT AND MATERIALS

I live in the country. It is pretty and peaceful, but it can also be frustrating. I am always running out of thread. With no stores for miles, I can spend half a day trying to find my thread rather than working on my quilt at home. There is a lesson in all of this: go over the following list carefully. Gather together everything on the list before you begin to work. The ones that are "must-have—no-substitute" are starred(*). You can make substitutes for the rest. Use your good common sense. As in any project, the most valuable thing you are investing in this quilt is your time. If you have to buy any of these supplies, buy the best you can afford.

heavy cardboard	Designer illustration or mat board is the best. Corrugated cardboard will not work. Posterboard or railroad board will work, but you will have to recut some templates as edges and corners get worn. Illustration board is sold in half or whole sheets; with careful spacing and cutting, a half sheet will be large enough to cut all the templates in this book.
***sharp** No. 2 pencil	
mat knife	This is the artist's term for the instrument you'll need to cut out the cardboard templates. It is sold in hardware stores and is called a "utility" knife. An X-ACTO knife will work, but I prefer the heftiness of the mat knife. If you already have one of these, treat it and yourself to a fresh, sharp blade. Do not use shears to cut out cardboard templates.
rubber cement	
scissors for cutting paper	
old magazine, cardboard or wallboard scrap	You need a cutting surface about 16″ × 20″ to protect your work area from your knife as you cut the templates.
colored pencils	
right angle triangle	Mine is metal and works well, although a plastic one is also suitable. It is used to line up tracing lines perpendicular to the selvage of the fabric so it is helpful to have one that is a little big (12″–18″) rather than one that is too small.
***metal ruler**	An 18″ ruler is a good all-purpose length. A yard ruler is also helpful. Be sure to check your ruler for accuracy. In quiltmaking, a quarter-inch must be exactly one quarter of an inch.
***shears**	Good sharp fabric shears are especially important. I have a nice lightweight pair that feel good in my hand. I keep the blades very sharp. Treat yourself—get yours sharpened before you begin your quilt. Then hide the shears from the kids—and don't let yourself be tempted to use them for anything except fabric either!
small plastic bags	Use these to organize your templates and your cut fabric pieces.
***needles**	Quilter's needles are called "betweens." Buy a package of assorted sizes.
pins	My pins are long, thin and sharp with glass heads. Avoid "horse pins." These are any that are fat and dull. They are hard on your fabric and your sewing machine.
***thimble**	If you have never used one, now is the very best time to learn. Find one that fits the middle finger of your sewing hand. Be stubborn about learning to sew with it. Otherwise, the very gentle art of quilting will also be very painful.
quilting hoop or frame	A quilting frame is a luxury for those with lots of space or a very understanding family. A hoop can work just as well as a frame. If you have a choice, choose a round hoop rather than an oval one.

HOW BIG DO YOU WANT YOUR QUILT TO BE?

Quilts are made for many places. The place a quilt is to be used determines how big it should be. Beds are standard sizes; blank walls are not. How do you decide what size is the best for you? Look at the table below. If you are making a quilt for a bed, fill in the blanks under the column that applies to you. If you are making a wall quilt, fill in the blanks under the "Other" column. Use the numbers given in the "Example" column as a guide. Quilts generally hang over three sides of a bed. They may or may not have an allowance for a pillow tuck. Old beds which sit high off the floor need more of an overhang than a contemporary waterbed. Keep special requirements that you have in mind as you fill in the chart.

Unless you have some special requirements, your ideal quilt size should match up closely with one of the four standard quilt sizes given on pages 6–7. (In an effort to design one "standard" quilt with 12″ blocks that can be adaptable to anyone making a quilt for a twin, double, queen or king-size bed, some allowances had to be made. Hence, the overhang varies from size to size. A pillow tuck allowance may or may not have been included.)

If your ideal size does not match up with one of the four given sizes, try to pick one of the given sizes that will work for you, keeping the following in mind:

(1) A good, but general guideline is to make your quilt a bit bigger than you need it rather than smaller.

(2) A quilt could be a little longer than you want it rather than not as wide as you need it.

(3) Try to match width measurements, and see if you can be satisfied with the length. This may mean that you have to have a pillow tuck when you didn't plan on one, or that you will have to use your quilt as a coverlet with shams.

The "standard" sampler quilt given here is a coverlet-type of quilt, hanging over the mattress ten to fourteen inches (depending on its size) on three sides. It can be used with a dust ruffle and pillow shams if you choose to do so.

If you absolutely have to make adjustments to one set of the given dimensions to suit your needs, try to make changes in the widths of the lattice strips or in the borders. Keep the block size twelve inches square. If you change the size of the block, the templates provided in the book cannot be used. If you have to make very large adjustments, try adding or substracting a row of blocks. Use graph paper to check your proportions and your figures.

My Ideal Quilt Dimensions

	TWIN	DOUBLE	EXAMPLE	QUEEN	KING	OTHER
Bed Size	39 × 75	54 × 75	54 × 75	60 × 80	72 × 80	__ ×
Drop/Overhang	__ × __	__ × __	12 × 12	__ × __	__ × __	__ × __
	__ × __	__ × __	12 × 0	__ × __	__ × __	__ × __
Pillow Tuck	__ × __	__ × __	_ × 12	__ × __	__ × __	__ × __
Take-up	+4 × +4	+4 × +4	+4 × +4	+4 × +4	+4 × +4	_+ × +_
Total (width × length)	__ × __	__ × __	82 × 103	__ × __	__ × __	__ × __

NOTE: All of these quilts have a built-in "take-up" allowance; this is to allow for the shrinkage in dimensions that occurs when a surface is quilted. If you change the given

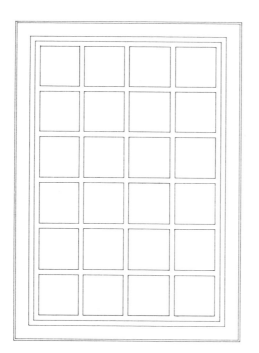

TWIN QUILT	67½″ × 94½″
No. of Blocks	4 across × 6 down = 24 total
Lattice	1½″ wide
Border	1½″ + 1½″ + 4″ = 7″ total width
Binding	½″ on all sides
Allowances	13″ overhang on 3 sides plus some extra length— but no full 12″ pillow tuck

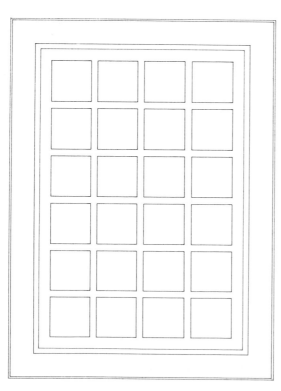

DOUBLE QUILT	79″ × 107″
No. of Blocks	4 across × 6 down = 24 total
Lattice	2″ wide
Border	3½″ + 1½″ + 7″ = 12″ total width
Binding	½″ on all sides
Allowances	13″–14″ overhang with 12″ pillow tuck

dimensions for any of these quilts, remember to add an extra two to four inches for this shrinkage to your desired length and width measurements.

QUEEN QUILT	85″ × 99″
No. of Blocks	5 across × 6 down = 30 total*
Lattice	2″ wide
Border	2″ + 2″ + 4″ = 8″ total width
Binding	½″ on all sides
Allowances	10″–11″ overhang with 12″ pillow tuck
*NOTE: To make 30 blocks, you must make 2 each of 6 of the blocks presented.	

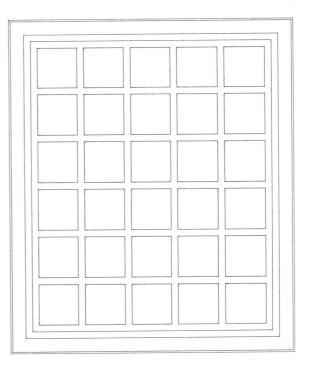

KING QUILT	99″ × 99″
No. of Blocks	6 across × 6 down = 36 total*
Lattice	2″ wide
Border	2″ + 2″ + 4″ = 8″ total width
Binding	½″ on all sides
Allowances	10″ overhang on 3 sides —no pillow tuck
*NOTE: To make 36 blocks, you must make 2 each of 12 of the blocks presented.	

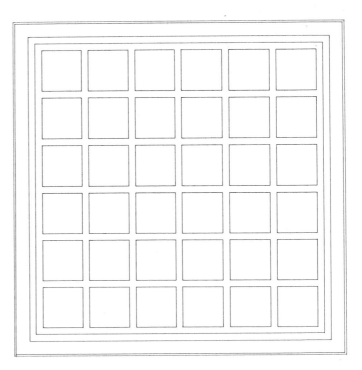

FABRICS

Contemporary quilts are made of almost anything that rolls off a bolt. Traditionally, quilts are made of dress-weight cotton. A good quilt fabric is one that is closely woven and has body. Most quilters prefer to use 100% cotton because it is soft, easy to sew and wears well. Cotton has a "give" that most synthetics do not; this "give" makes it simpler to ease in fullness when trying to match corners and edges.

I love to work with cotton, and use it any time I can. Sometimes, though, there is a print or color that is just what I want and—you guessed it—it isn't all cotton. I may decide to use it anyway. As a general rule, try to limit your choices to those fabrics that are at least 70% cotton. And, whenever you are trying to choose between two fabrics, choose the one with the highest cotton content. Be sure to avoid using knits or loosely woven fabrics of any kind.

For many quilters, settling on an acceptable fabric content is the easy part when choosing fabrics for a quilt. Don't let a dazzling array of prints and colors intimidate you. Making fabric choices is fun. Relax and enjoy it. If you find that having so many choices is confusing, let me give you a few guidelines to help.

Six different fabrics is a good number to use to make your sampler quilt. There will be enough possibilities to give you a variety of combinations, but not too many to be frustrating. If you are confident in your ability to blend many prints and colors, feel free to use more than six. To start, pick one fabric that you would especially like to use in your quilt. Pull it out of the rack and set it aside. Then choose three more fabrics that coordinate with your first choice. Pull them out of the rack and stack them on top of your first fabric. How do they look? Try to vary the scale of your prints. Notice how some very small prints can really be used instead of solid colors. Have you chosen a large-scale print? Sometimes these can give a fresh look to a quilt. How will it look when cut into small pieces? Will you still like it? What is missing? Choose a fifth fabric. Do you need a bright color? a light color? a print that will provide a contrast to your other four choices? You may want to choose a solid-colored fabric as your sixth choice to use in your border and lattice. Before you buy your fabric, decide which one of the six will be used for your border and lattice—this fabric will frame each block and set it off from the rest. As a final test, stand back from your fabric choices and look again. Be sure that you like the way they look from ten feet away as well as you do from up close.

Some Last Bits of Advice About Shopping for Fabrics

Buy the best quality that you can afford. These days, your time is worth as much as your money. This does not mean that the higher the price of the fabric, the better the quality. Use your judgment and the guidelines above. If you are on a budget, search out remnant tables and other likely locations for less expensive but good-quality fabric.

You may not find all the fabrics for your quilt at one place. Take the whole piece of fabric with you when you shop to find another to go with it; a little swatch really doesn't help much. And you will never remember just what shade of green a print is when it is home on your sewing table.

Shop with an open mind. You aren't buying fabric for a dress. You may choose a print or a color that you would never consider wearing. Trust your instincts. When you get home and start to cut and sew, you may find that one of your fabrics isn't working, that you avoid using it. Then don't. Choose another. This happens to the best of us. Even though it doesn't work in this quilt, it may be just the fabric you need for another.

Finally, be sure to buy as much of each fabric as you think you will need. If you suspect that you will use more of one fabric than you will of another, buy a bit more of the first and less of the second. Fabrics come and go. Even if you can find that certain print a month later, it is often from another dye lot—and may not match yours at all. If it is very important to you that your quilt back be one of the six fabrics that you have chosen, you should buy it at the same time as you buy the rest. I often use an unrelated print or a plain muslin back on my quilts. I delay buying the fabric for the back until I need it. This is one way to spread the total cost of the quilt over a period of time.

How Much to Buy?

Figuring out how much fabric to buy is easy. I have done all the math for you! If you are not making a quilt that is one of the four given sizes, you will have to do some figuring on your own. If your quilt dimensions fall between two of the ones given, make a "guess-timate": consider how much fabric each of those requires, and pick an amount somewhere between the two. It is best not to piece the long border strips (though you can do it if you have to), so you might consider buying one of your fabrics at least the length of your quilt.

Feel free to make adjustments in the yardage requirements suggested for the fabrics you decide to use in your blocks. As long as your total yardage equals that of the suggested amounts, you will have enough fabric to complete your top. Fabric requirements given for the border and lattice, though, are minimum amounts and should not be reduced.

When you are purchasing your fabric, be sure to choose your thread. One or two large spools should be plenty. You can sew together your entire top using the same color. Pick one that will blend with all of your fabrics. Choose a lighter color rather than a darker one if you must make that kind of choice. I often use off-white when piecing any light to medium-toned quilt top. If your fabric is 100% cotton, use all-cotton thread if you can find it. Otherwise use cotton-covered polyester thread.

QUILT YARDAGE REQUIREMENTS
using 45"-wide fabric

	TWIN	DOUBLE	QUEEN	KING
Border & Lattice (includes enough fabric to use in blocks also; no need to add to this amount for use in blocks)	3¾ yds.	5 yds.	5⅜ yds.	5½ yds.
Blocks (yardage for each of the 5 other fabrics)	1½ yds.	1½ yds.	2 yds.	2¼ yds.
Binding	½ yd.	½ yd.	½ yd.	⅝ yd.
Back	5¾* yds.	6½* yds.	6 yds.	8¾ yds.

*If the fabric that you plan to use for your quilt back is also one that you want to use in your blocks, you do not have to buy the suggested amount listed for this one fabric in the "Blocks" column.

But you will have to pre-measure and pre-cut your back to make the excess fabric available for use in your blocks. Allow a margin of several inches around all sides of your top's measurements when measuring and cutting.

PREPARING YOUR FABRIC FOR CUTTING

All of your fabrics must be washed before you begin to use them. Some may shrink; others may not be colorfast. If you have a fabric that you suspect is not colorfast (dark blues and reds are famous for this), plan to wash it separately from the others. Wash it until no more color runs —or plan on never washing your quilt again. (Having your quilt dry-cleaned is an option—more about that on page 46.)

Before you wash your fabrics, clip along the selvage edges every four inches along the entire length of each fabric. This will help keep the grain straight if any shrinkage does occur. Then wash your fabrics as you will wash your completed quilt. Some say to use the hottest water that you dare. Others insist that only warm water and a mild detergent should be used. Use your judgment.

Hang your fabrics to dry. Drying long lengths of fabric in the dryer can pull and twist the grain completely out of line. When your fabric is dry, check the grainlines. The crosswise threads should be perpendicular to the lengthwise threads. If they are not, straighten the grainlines by pulling on the true bias along the selvage edges; see *Diagram 1.*

Press your fabrics to remove any wrinkles. They are now ready to use.

MAKING TEMPLATES

A template is a cardboard or plastic shape that a quilter uses to transfer parts of a patchwork pattern onto fabric by tracing around the edges. If a quilter sews by hand, the template should not include a seam allowance; the traced line is the *sewing* line and the seam allowance is added when cutting out the pieces. If the quilter sews by machine, the template should include the seam allowance; the traced line is the *cutting* line. For this quilt, I assume that you will be piecing your blocks by machine. (If you want to piece your quilt by hand, you can still use the templates provided. Refer to a more comprehensive quilting book for directions on hand piecing.)

Cut the template pages out of your book. (If you are a person who just can't bear to cut up a book, trace each shape onto graph paper very carefully. Use the lines on the paper as a guide to keep the shapes accurate.) Cutting freehand, separate each shape from the others. Do not cut on the printed lines; leave some blank space around each one as you cut. Using rubber cement, glue each of your shapes onto heavy cardboard. I like to use artist's mat board. Other likely substitutes are listed in your supply list. Cutting the templates out will be much easier if you leave some space between each shape as you glue; see *Diagram 2.*

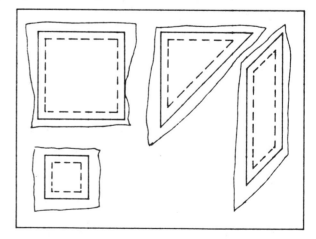

Diagram 2. *Using rubber cement, glue each of your templates onto heavy cardboard, leaving some space between each shape for easier cutting.*

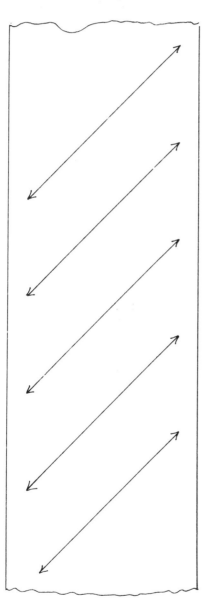

Diagram 1. *The arrows represent the fabric's "true" bias. Pull on the true bias along the length of your fabric to straighten wavy or crooked grainlines.*

Beginning at this point, and from this point until you have pieced the complete quilt top, accuracy is absolutely essential. If there is any rule in quiltmaking, this is it: **BE ACCURATE.** It is not hard. Work slowly and carefully. It will become a habit. If you are tired and don't really want to work on your quilt, don't. Many find that piecing is relaxing and a joy—but that is only because they have made a habit of working accurately.

If you have never used an X-ACTO knife or mat knife to cut cardboard, make a few practice cuts. Be sure to protect your cutting surface with an old magazine or scrap of heavy cardboard. Draw several pencil lines on one end of your cardboard; draw a shape or two. Place your metal ruler along one of these practice lines. Hold the ruler firmly so that it will not slip. Draw the blade of your knife along the ruler's edge. Do not try to cut through the cardboard with the first pass. Continue to hold the ruler firmly against the cardboard. Draw the blade along the edge of the ruler again, pressing down on your knife slightly harder than you did the first time. If necessary, do it a third time. If you still have not cut through the board, check to be sure that your blade is sharp, and replace it if necessary.

After you feel confident cutting with your knife, cut out all of your templates. Handle them carefully. Damaged points and rough edges don't produce accurate shapes. All the care possible has been taken to print these templates accurately, so check your cut pieces against graph paper to be sure yours are accurate.

A Note on Plastic Templates

Plastic templates can be very useful when you want to cut your fabric in a specific way. For instance, you may want to center a flower in the middle of a square or cut away a certain section of a floral stripe. Hobby shops and quilt shops sell heavyweight acetate sheets that are good for making quilter's templates. Trace the shape of your template onto the plastic; use your knife and metal ruler to cut it out. Use care when you are tracing around a plastic template on your fabric—its surface is often slick and the template can slide as you trace. Putting several small pieces of masking or other textured tape onto the underside of your template can help minimize slippage.

MARKING OFF AND CUTTING BORDER, LATTICE AND BINDING STRIPS

Before you can use any of your templates to trace pieces for your blocks, you must mark off and cut away the fabric that you will need for your borders and lattice. If it is important to you that a certain fabric be used as the binding, you should cut it out at this time too.

If you are making one of the four standard quilt sizes, simply consult the Table of Lengths and Widths on page 12 to determine the length and width of the strips you need for the size you have chosen to make. These mea-

surements all include your ¼″ seam allowance. If you have adjusted one of the given quilt dimensions by changing border and lattice sizes, be sure to keep those changes in mind as you measure and cut. Also, be certain that you have added the ¼″ seam allowance to your adjusted lengths and widths. If you have graphed out your adjustments, consult your graph. If you haven't and feel uncertain of your figures, it might be a good idea to graph your adjustments now.

When cutting, start with the fabric that you have chosen for the outer border strips. Lay the fabric flat on your table. You must cut away the selvage; it is never used—even when it would be hidden in the seam allowance. So that you will not waste any fabric, use a right angle and a metal ruler to draw a right-angle corner in the bottom left corner of your fabric, as shown in *Diagram 3*. The vertical side of the corner will be about ½″ from the selvage edge. Depending on how straight your fabric was cut when you bought it, the horizontal side of the corner will be anywhere from ½″ to several inches from the cut edge of your fabric. Your pencilled right angle should correspond with the lengthwise and crosswise threads (grain) of your fabric.

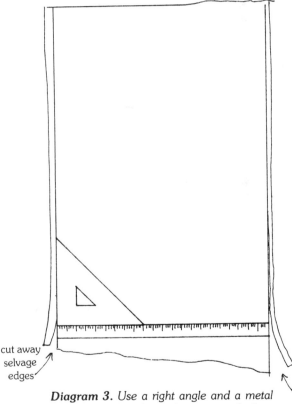

cut away selvage edges

Diagram 3. Use a right angle and a metal ruler to draw a right-angle corner in the bottom left corner of your fabric.

Use the pencilled line along the selvage as the left edge of your first border strip. Measure across the width of your fabric, ticking off the widths of the remaining three outer borders as you move up the fabric to achieve the length. Connect your marks with a very sharp pencil, making straight lines. When you have measured out the length and width of the four outer borders, cut them away from the fabric and set them aside. Repeat this procedure to cut the inner borders from the same fabric.

Look at the line drawing of the sampler quilt *(Diagram 5)* on page 14. The strips of fabric that "frame" each of the blocks are called the lattice strips or sashes. Measure and cut these sashes from the same fabric that you have used to cut your outer and inner borders.

The Table of Lengths and Widths on this page gives two sets of measurements for the sashes. The long sashes are horizontal; measure and cut these first. The vertical sashes are short in length. Add up the total length of fabric that you'll need for the short strips; for example, if you are making a double-size quilt, you would multiply $16 \times 12\frac{1}{2}''$ for a total of 200″. Obviously you wouldn't have enough yardage to cut this strip in one piece, but you can divide that measurement into workable lengths and cut strips of those lengths from your fabric. Then use your sash template on Plate O or P to mark off these strips into the short lengths. Also, you will find that you may be able to utilize the leftover ends cut away from the long sashes for some of these short sashes.

Look at the line drawing again. Choose the fabric you would like to use for the narrow contrasting strip—the middle border. Measure and cut these strips. You may cut as many as you need to add up to the total given in the chart.

If you are certain at this point about the fabric you want to use to bind your quilt, measure and cut it out also. I often leave this until last because I am usually not sure which fabric will work best until the quilt top is finished. Often I use a fabric for the binding that was not used in the quilt. However, if you don't measure out your

TABLE OF LENGTHS* AND WIDTHS OF ALL BORDER, LATTICE AND BINDING STRIPS FOR THE FOUR STANDARD QUILT SIZES

	TWIN	DOUBLE	QUEEN	KING
Outer Border	2—4½″ × 95″ 2—4½″ × 68″	2—7½″ × 108″ 2—7½″ × 80″	2—4½″ × 99½″ 2—4½″ × 85½″	4—4½″ × 99½″
Middle Border	2—2″ × 86″ 2—2″ × 59″	2—2″ × 92½″ 2—2″ × 64½″	2—2½″ × 90½″ 2—2½″ × 76½″	4—2½″ × 90½″
Inner Border	2—2″ × 83″ 2—2″ × 57½″	2—4″ × 89½″ 2—4″ × 61½″	2—2½″ × 84½″ 2—2½″ × 72½″	4—2½″ × 86½″
Long Sashes	5—2″ × 53″	5—2½″ × 54½″	5—2½″ × 68½″	5—2½″ × 82½″
Short Sashes	16—2″ × 12½″	16—2½″ × 12½″	24—2½″ × 12½″	30—2½″ × 12½″
Binding	2″ wide × 326″	2″ wide × 372″	2″ wide × 368″	2″ wide × 396″

*Lengths given here are exactly what you will need if you work absolutely accurately. On all *except* the short 12½″ sashes, allow yourself an additional several inches whenever you can as a safety margin.

binding now and set it aside, it is possible that you will have to find another fabric for your binding. As an alternative, you can keep in mind that you will need to save the binding yardage amount of one of your fabrics given in the Table of Lengths and Widths. When you have cut and pieced about half of your blocks, and have a better idea which fabric will look best as a binding, you can measure and set it aside then. These strips will have to be pieced in any case. Just remember to leave enough of one fabric to do the job. (Binding does not have to be cut on the bias when finishing straight edges—more on that on page 46.)

RELATIONSHIPS—SHADES, COLORS, TEXTURES

Look carefully at each of the finished sampler quilts on the covers of this book. It is hard to believe that all five are the same quilt—made up of the same twenty-four blocks that you are about to make. Why is each quilt so different from the others? An obvious difference is that each is made using a different color combination. But look more closely. Pick out one block and locate it in each of the quilts. Is the dark square in that one dark in all the rest? What about the light triangle? Is there one fabric in each quilt that has been used more than the rest? Is there one fabric that seems to dominate the rest? What is the result?

Most patchwork patterns are very simple. It is the relationships created between lights and darks, the interplay of colors, and the variety of textures offered by differently scaled prints that make them dynamic and appear to be complex.

Pages 16–31 are the "coloring" section of your book. Each of the twenty-four blocks in the sampler quilt is illustrated by six drawings: two that I have "colored" and four for you to color. They are presented in a suggested working order—beginning with "very easy" and ending with "interesting."

Choose six colored pencils to represent the fabrics you have chosen for your quilt. Examine the first two drawings that I have "colored"; refer to *Diagram 4* for an explanation of each of the different shadings. Then, using your pencils, color the four blank drawings, each in a different way. Experiment. Pick the one that you like the best and mark it with a star or check. That will be the combination that you will use in your quilt.

Continue to color in the blank illustrations of each of the blocks. This can be rather time-consuming, and is good "T.V." work. ("T.V." work is any work that can be done while some other activity is going on around you. Cutting out traced pieces is also good "T.V." work . . . .) If you are impatient to begin sewing, color in five or six of the blocks. When you trace and sew, you will have enough combinations to do several at a time. Don't try to piece a block that you haven't colored. Erasing a pencilled block is much quicker and easier than recutting pieces or ripping out seams.

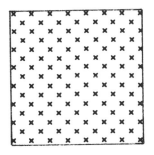

A small-scale print with a high value, i.e. light in color. Such a print can often be used in place of a solid color.

A medium-scale print with a low value, i.e., dark in color.

A medium-scale print with a medium value. A multi-colored quilt usually has several medium-scale/medium-value prints.

A large-scale print with a medium value. The regular repeat of motifs in a large print can lend itself to creative cutting to "frame" certain parts of the design.

Diagram 4. *Guide to the different scales and values of fabric prints used in the Coloring Section on pages 16–31.*

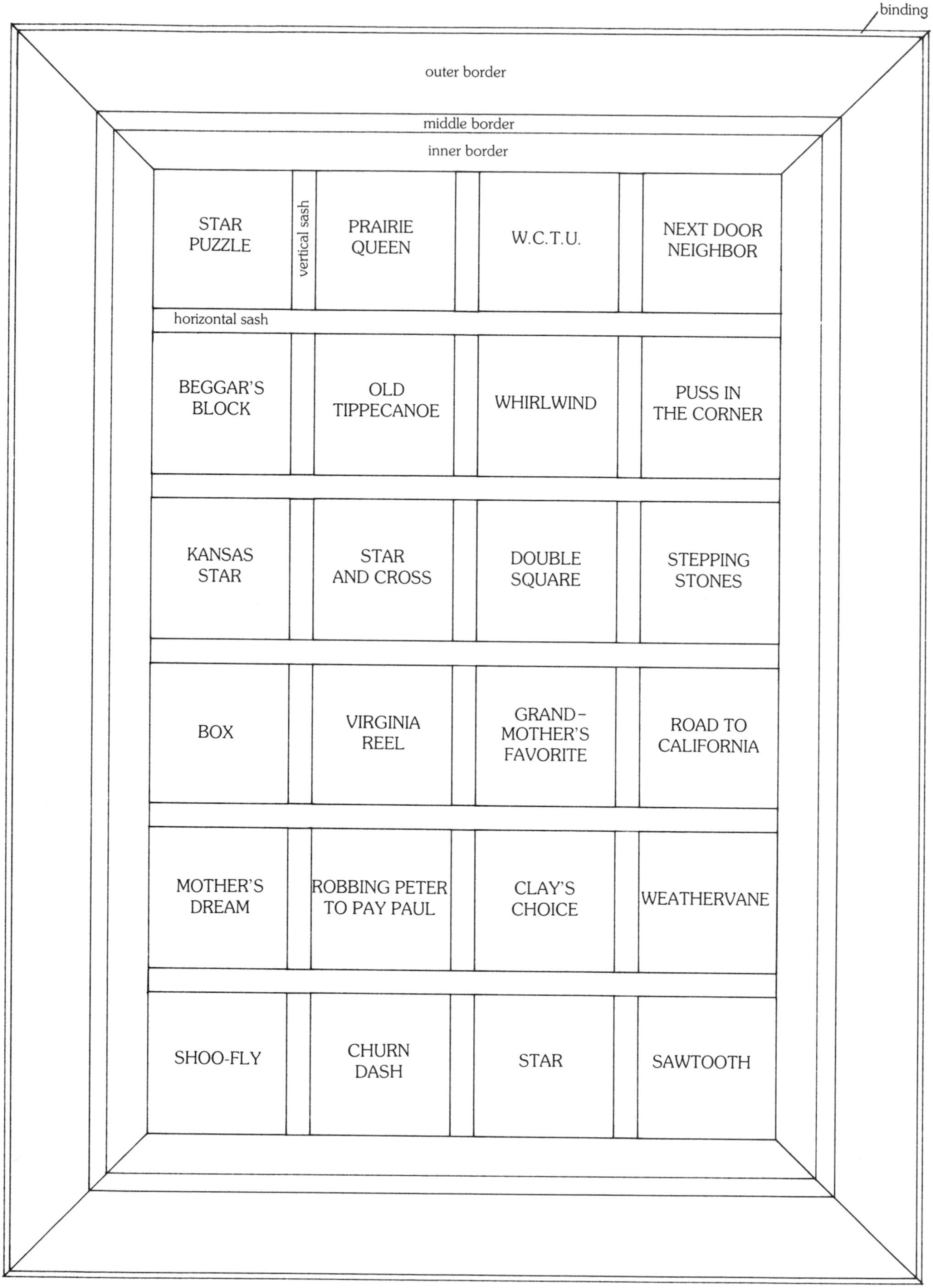

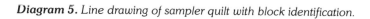

binding

outer border

middle border

inner border

	vertical sash			
STAR PUZZLE		PRAIRIE QUEEN	W.C.T.U.	NEXT DOOR NEIGHBOR

horizontal sash

BEGGAR'S BLOCK	OLD TIPPECANOE	WHIRLWIND	PUSS IN THE CORNER
KANSAS STAR	STAR AND CROSS	DOUBLE SQUARE	STEPPING STONES
BOX	VIRGINIA REEL	GRAND-MOTHER'S FAVORITE	ROAD TO CALIFORNIA
MOTHER'S DREAM	ROBBING PETER TO PAY PAUL	CLAY'S CHOICE	WEATHERVANE
SHOO-FLY	CHURN DASH	STAR	SAWTOOTH

Diagram 5. *Line drawing of sampler quilt with block identification.*

Diagram 6. *Line drawing of sampler quilt; refer to* Diagram 5 *for block identification.*

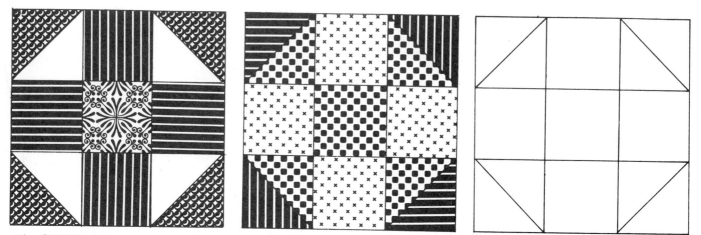

#1   SHOO-FLY

#2   CHURN DASH

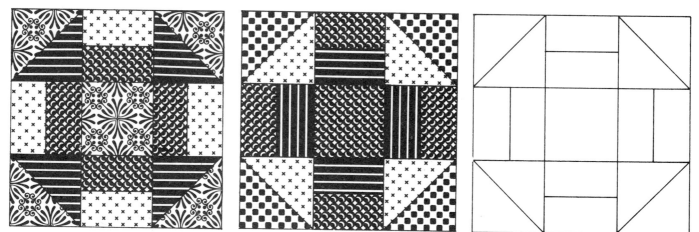

#3   STAR

16

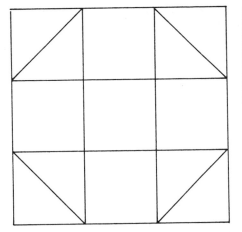 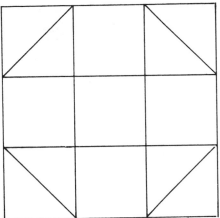 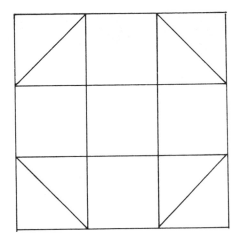

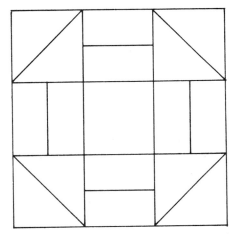 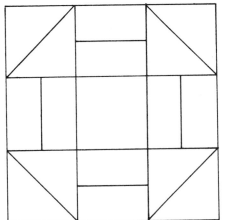 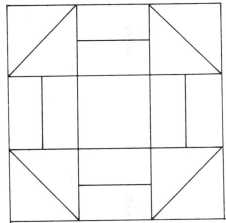

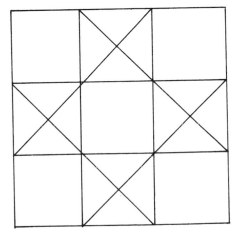 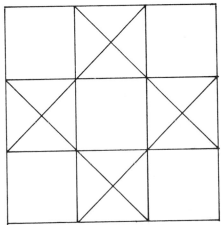 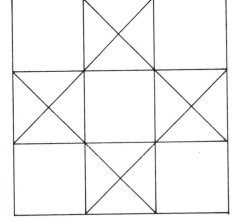

#4 PRAIRIE QUEEN

#5 W.C.T.U.

#6 MOTHER'S DREAM

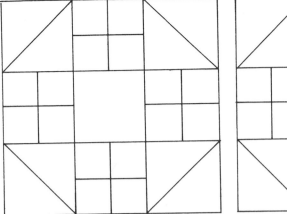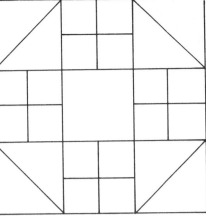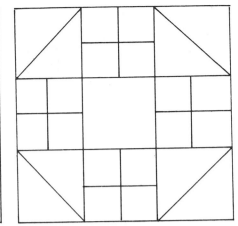

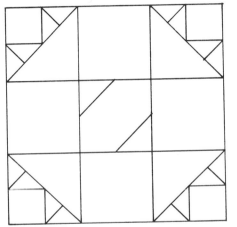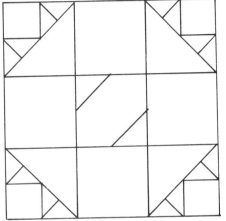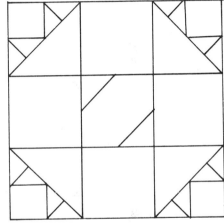

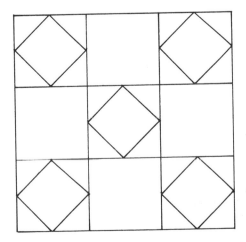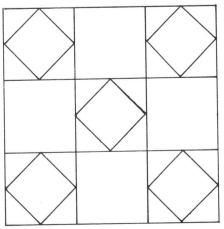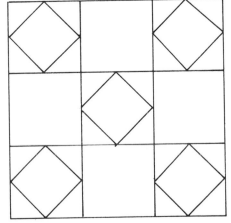

#7   WHIRLWIND

#8   BEGGAR'S BLOCK

#9   ROAD TO CALIFORNIA

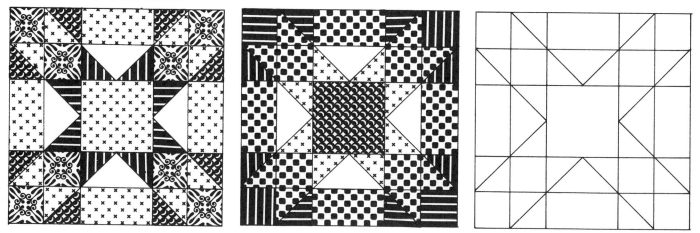

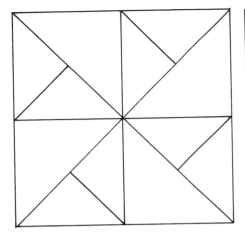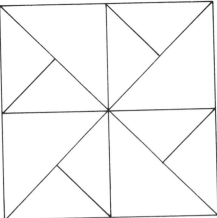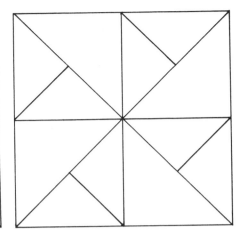

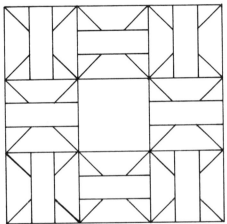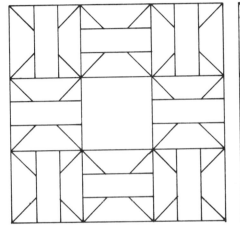

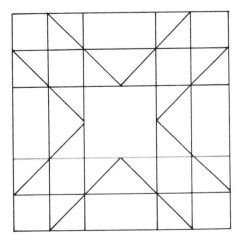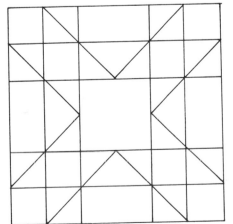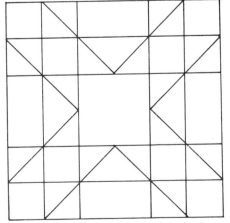

#10 SAWTOOTH

#11 STEPPING STONES

#12 ROBBING PETER TO PAY PAUL

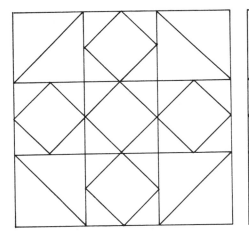 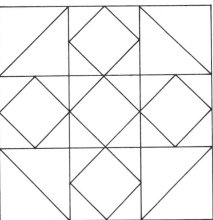 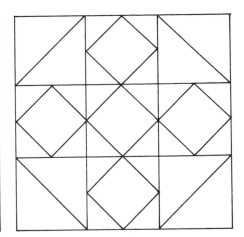

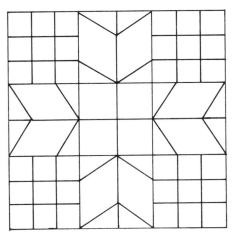 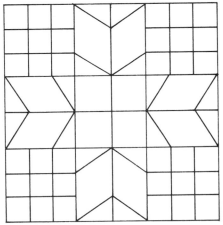 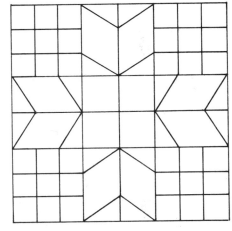

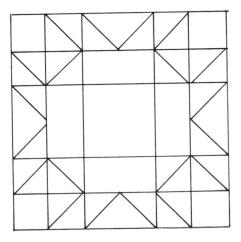 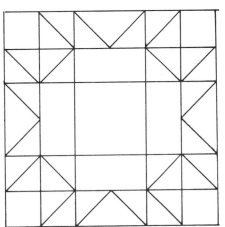 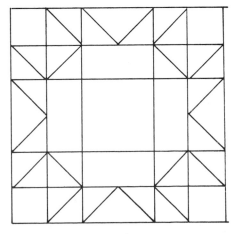

#13   WEATHERVANE

#14   KANSAS STAR

#15   GRANDMOTHER'S FAVORITE

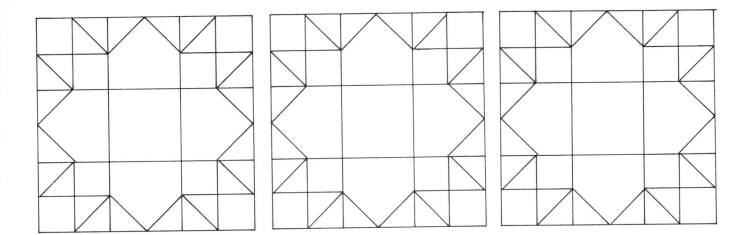

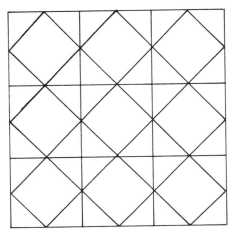
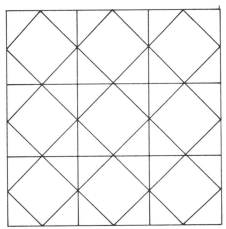
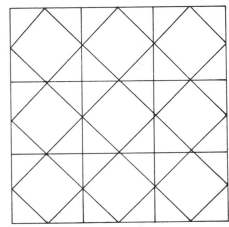

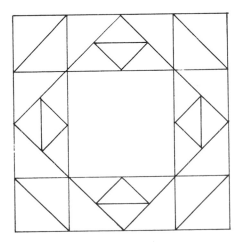
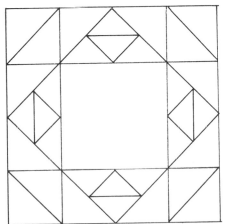
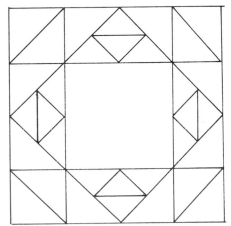

#16 OLD TIPPECANOE

#17 NEXT DOOR NEIGHBOR

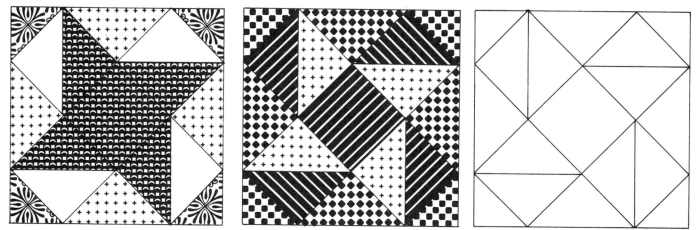

#18 DOUBLE SQUARE

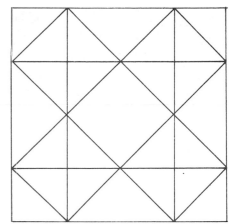
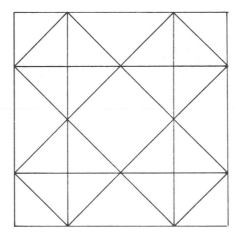

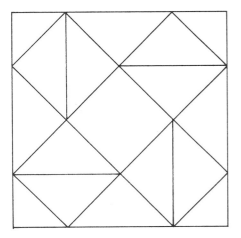
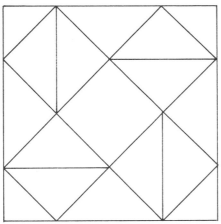
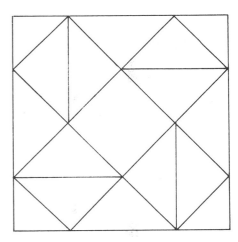
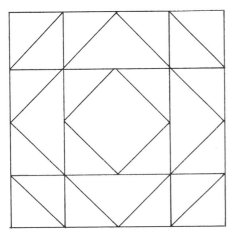
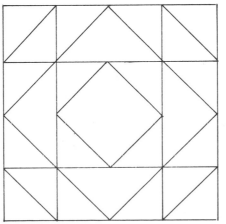
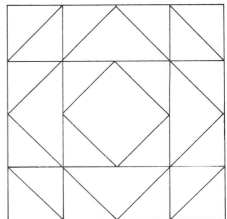

#19   STAR PUZZLE

#20   VIRGINIA REEL

#21   STAR AND CROSS

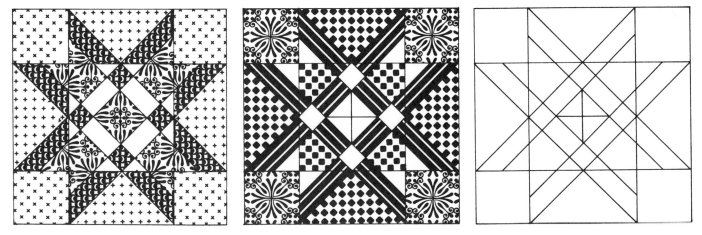

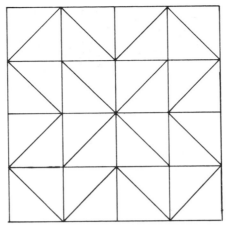
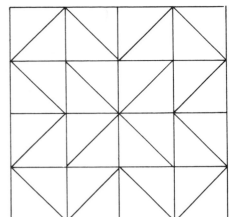

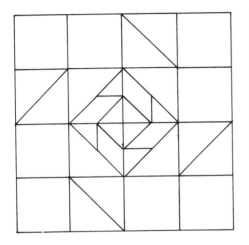
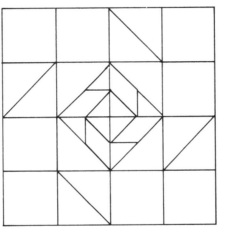
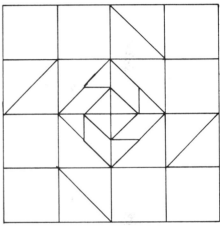

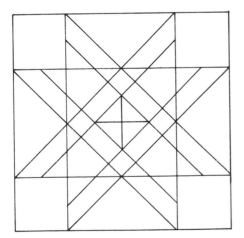
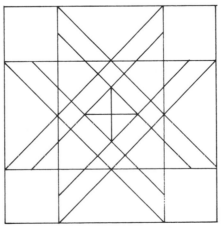
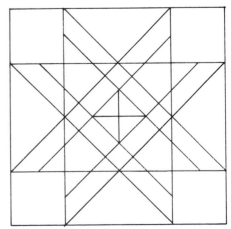

#22 CLAY'S CHOICE

#23 PUSS IN THE CORNER

#24 BOX

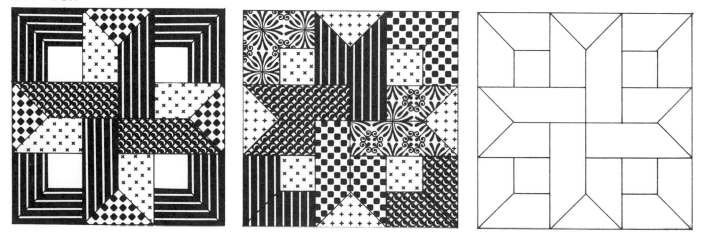

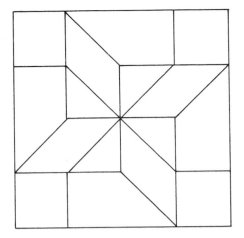 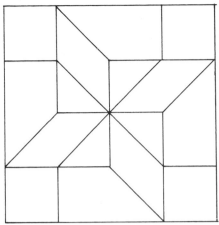 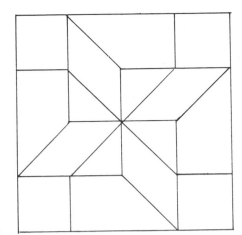

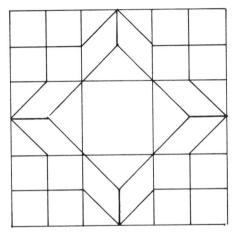 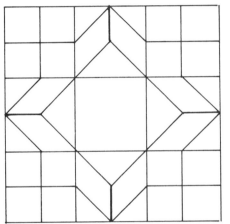 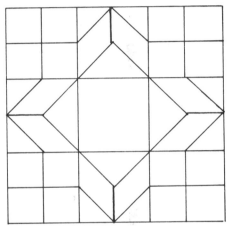

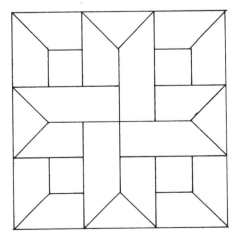 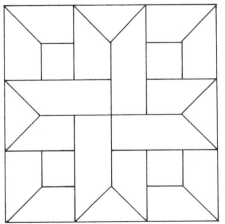 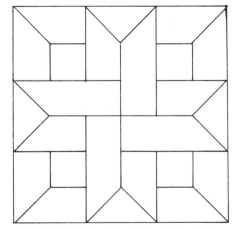

HOW TO TRACE AND CUT

Before tracing any shapes for your blocks onto the fabric, iron the fabric. Be sure to use the right setting for the fabric content. Don't push on your iron as you press—this will pull your fabric off the straight grain.

I have discussed grainlines before, but now is when you really have to give them some thought. The grainlines of any woven fabric are made up of the threads with which it is woven; see *Diagram 7*. The crosswise grain goes from selvage to selvage, which is the woven edge found along two sides of the fabric. If you pull on a fabric along the crosswise grain, it will stretch a little. The lengthwise grain runs parallel to the selvage, usually from cut end to cut end if you have purchased the fabric from a bolt. There is no stretch along the lengthwise grain. The true bias of a fabric runs along the intersection of the cross and lengthwise grainlines at a 45° angle to the selvage. The maximum stretch in a given fabric is along the true bias. (Keep this last fact in mind as you sew: the stretch of the bias can work for you . . . and against you.)

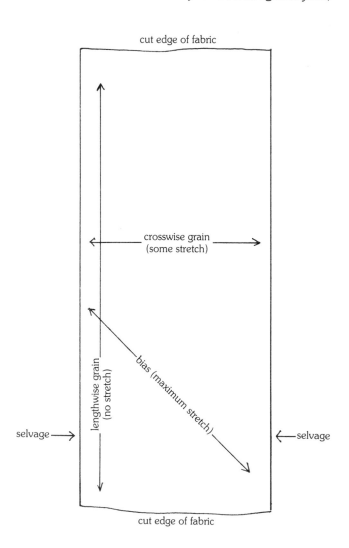

Diagram 7. The grainlines of a piece of woven fabric.

Let's start with an easy block and go through the tracing and cutting process step by step. Pull out the templates that you will need for the Shoo-Fly *(Diagram 8)*; the templates (#1 and #2) can be found on Plate A. You'll be working with a medium-sized triangle and a square. You have already chosen the colors for this block. Check back to the colored drawing you have selected on page 16 or 17. Pull out the fabric that you have chosen for the squares. You may need five squares of one color, or four of one and one of a second, depending on how you have colored your block.

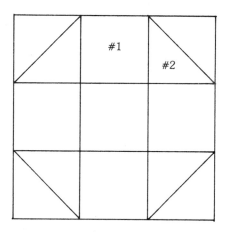

Diagram 8. The simplest quilt block in this book—the Shoo-Fly design.

Lay out your fabric right side up to trace your shapes. This is contrary to the way that many quilters work, always tracing on the wrong side of the fabric. I like to see exactly where on a print my pencil line is moving. On a very dark print, however, it is easier to see your cutting lines when they are drawn on the wrong side of the fabric.

With a metal straightedge placed parallel to the selvage, and about ¼″ to ½″ from it, draw a vertical line along the entire length of the ruler as shown in *Diagram 9*. Butt the corner of your right triangle along this penciled line, as close to the cut edge of the fabric as possible. If your fabric was cut along the grain in the store, this line will be very close to the cut edge; if your fabric was not cut straight, you may lose an inch or more along this edge. Trace a line along the bottom edge of your triangle as shown in *Diagram 10*. This line will be absolutely perpendicular to your first line. Use your straightedge to extend this horizontal line across the entire width of your fabric following *Diagram 11*. Each of these lines will be on a grainline: the first along the lengthwise grain; the second, along the crosswise grain. (This all sounds more complicated than it really is. All you are doing is drawing two straight and perpendicular lines to correct for a wavy selvage and a crooked cut edge in the bottom left corner of your fabric.)

Since this quilt was designed to be sewn on the machine, the line that you trace around each of your templates is your cutting line. Pick up your square template #1. Place it in the corner that you have just made with your two lines. With a pencil or washable pen (test it first), trace around the square's other two sides. If you are using a pencil, be sure to keep it sharp. Believe it or not, the thickness of a stubby pencil point can thwart your efforts for accuracy right from the start. Keep your pencil as close to the template as possible as you trace around it. Work as slowly as you must to be accurate.

Having common cutting lines between shapes wherever possible will save you both fabric and cutting time. To trace a second square, slide your template to the right, lining up the bottom left corner of the template with the right side of your first square and your long horizontal line. Be sure to position it perfectly. Then trace around the top and right edge of the template. Continue in this way until you have traced all the squares you will need for the block from this fabric. Then set the fabric aside.

If you have decided to make the center square of the block from a second fabric, pull out that fabric, and lay it flat on your table. Correct for wavy selvages and crooked cut edges as you did for your first fabric, by drawing the long perpendicular lines along the selvage and across the width. Trace the square and set the fabric aside.

Refer back to your color drawing of the block. How have you colored the triangles? Do you need four of one color and four more of a second? Pull out the fabric that you have chosen for one set of triangles. Lay it flat on your table and determine your "starting" corner as you did above.

Look at your triangle template. Notice the lines with the arrows printed on them? One of these lines must be parallel to a crosswise or lengthwise grain every time you trace around it. The long side of the triangle must always be on the true bias. This is no problem if you keep the other two sides of the triangle on the straight of the grain. Place the right angle of the triangle into the corner that you have drawn in the bottom left corner of your fabric. Be accurate. Trace along the long side of the triangle (the hypotenuse). Turn the template clockwise and align the long side of the template with the line that you have just drawn, matching the corners of the template to the corners of the triangle already drawn. Trace around the top and side of the triangle. Turn your template clockwise again, matching one side of the template to the side of the triangle that you have just traced, and keeping the bottom edge of the template along your long horizontal line. Trace along the long side of the triangle. Turn the template clockwise again, match the long side of the triangle and its corners, and trace a fourth triangle; see Diagram 12.

Check back to your color drawing. Perhaps the other set of four triangles is from one of the fabrics that you have already used for a square. If so, pull out that fabric again and lay it out flat. Keep in mind that you would

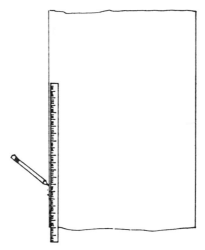

Diagram 9. Place a metal straightedge parallel to the selvage and about 1/4" to 1/2" from it.

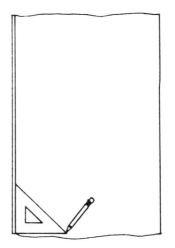

Diagram 10. Butt the corner of a right triangle along the pencilled selvage line and trace a line along the bottom edge of the triangle.

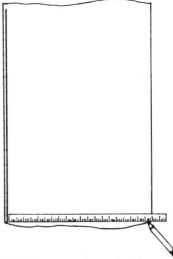

Diagram 11. Use a metal straightedge to extend the horizontal line across the entire width of the fabric.

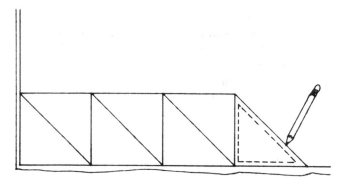

Diagram 12. Having common cutting lines between shapes will save both fabric and cutting time.

like to have as many common cutting lines as possible. Also, remember that you want the printed arrow to be parallel to the straight grain. Butt the right angle corner of the triangle into the corner made by the right side of the traced square and your long horizontal line. Trace along the long edge of the triangle. Continue to trace out as many triangles as you need of this fabric, as you did above.

Lots of words for a very simple process . . . just work carefully . . . accurately. At this point, I would probably trace the shapes I needed for four or five more blocks before I did any cutting. It saves time and trouble. If you can put off sewing for just a big longer, refer back to your colored drawings and trace the pieces you will need for the next several blocks: Churn Dash, Star, Prairie Queen and W.C.T.U. Continue to use your long horizontal and vertical lines as a guide to keep your shapes on the straight grain.

Cut out your shapes as carefully as you have traced them. Use sharp shears. (I have a lightweight pair that I use just for cutting quilt pieces. I never use them for any other cutting job—not even to cut thread.) Be sure to cut right through the center of your pencil line. Do not cut along one side of it.

Keep the pieces for each block separate from the rest. If this is going to be a long-term project, put the pieces for each block into separate plastic bags and label them.

PIECING AND PRESSING

"Why do you want to cut up perfectly good fabric into little pieces and then sew them back together again?" is a query often made by those who haven't discovered the joy of patchwork. From bits and pieces materializes something all-of-a-piece that is far more wonderful than the sometimes pedestrian fabric one had at the start.

Lay out the pieces for the Shoo-Fly block. Keep your colored drawing close at hand. Thread your machine (the same color thread can be used for all piecing), set your stitch length to 10–12 stitches-per-inch, and treat your machine to a new, sharp needle. Measure the dis-

tance between your needle and the right edge of your presser foot. If it is exactly ¼", you are ready to sew. If it is not, mark a ¼" seam allowance by taping a marked length of masking tape to your machine throat plate.

Look at the Shoo-Fly block. Do you see how the block is actually made up of nine smaller squares, arranged in a grid of three across and three down? Any pattern with this arrangement is called a "nine-patch." Most of the blocks in this quilt are nine-patch patterns. (That is why so many of the templates are interchangeable among the different blocks.) The blocks in this quilt that are not nine-patches are "four-patches"; see *Diagram 13*. Sometimes you have to look carefully at a block to figure out how it could possibly have been sewn together—which piece should be sewn to which piece first? But figuring out how to piece the Shoo-Fly isn't hard at all.

Start with the triangles. Look at your drawing. Pick up one each of the two sets that you have cut. With right sides facing, match the long sides of the triangles. Corners must match. Edges must match. Pin, if you feel you need to. With the needle raised, put the presser foot

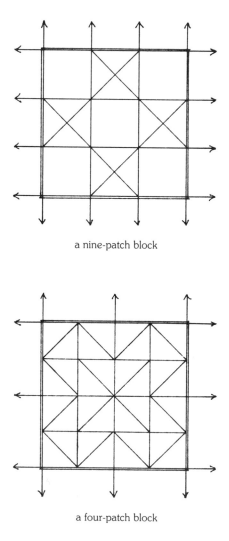

a nine-patch block

a four-patch block

Diagram 13. Compare the differences between nine-patch and four-patch blocks.

down and line up the edge of the seam to be sewn with your presser foot (or your ¼″ seam marked on tape). Starting to sew slowly, let the feed dogs pull your triangles into position under the presser foot, and sew the seam; do not break the thread. This is a seam sewn on the bias of both pieces. Be careful not to pull on the seam as you sew or you will stretch it. It is not necessary to backstitch. Pick up the next set of triangles, match edges and corners, position them, and stitch the seam. Sew your remaining two sets of triangles in the same way. When all have been stitched together, lift your presser foot, cut your thread and cut the threads joining the sets of triangles together. This process is called chain piecing; see *Diagram 14*. Using this process saves time, energy (it gets tiring raising and lowering the presser foot constantly) and thread. Do it any time you can.

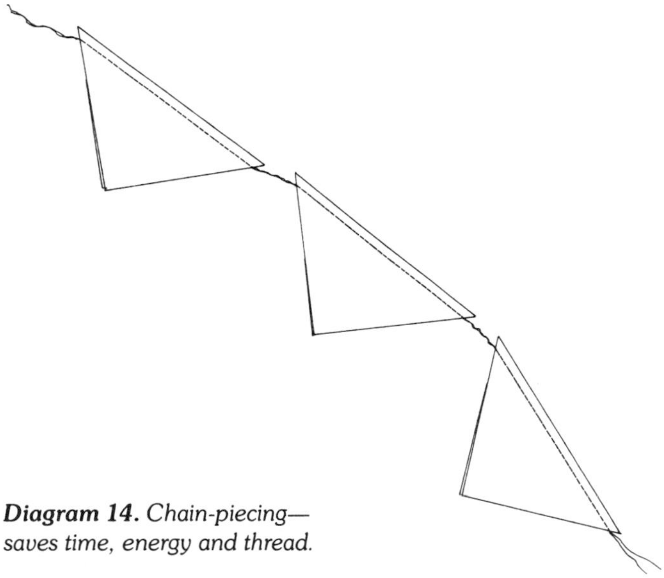

Diagram 14. Chain-piecing—
saves time, energy and thread.

Every seam must be pressed flat before another piece is sewn to it. Press with the hottest iron setting your fabric content will allow. Unlike seams in most other sewing, the seams in patchwork are not pressed open. This weakens your stitching. Instead, both seam allowances are pressed to one side.

Which side, you wonder? There are no rules, just general guidelines. Look at the block you are about to piece. Where will you quilt? If you are going to outline-quilt, stitching around parts of a pattern along the seam lines, press the seam allowance away from the edge you want to quilt. Press seam allowances away from very light-colored patches and, generally, toward dark ones. Press away from already bulky joints in previously sewn seams.

Lay out the nine small squares for the block, referring to your colored drawing. The next step is to sew the three sets of squares into rows. Whenever shapes are sewn together, points and corners must match perfectly. Look at your drawing. Keeping in mind that there is a ¼″ seam allowance around the outside edge of your still imaginary block, do you see that the points of the triangles must be

stitched right at the seam line, and not be hidden somewhere in it? You can insure that this will happen if you pin-baste. Put the point of your pin exactly where you intend to stitch, and then take care as you sew to stitch just where your pin indicates. To be more specific, pick up the top left square and the top center square of the block. With the top center square on top, put the tip of your pin in the intersection of the two ¼″ seam allowances on each side of the corner. Push the pin through the square, then put the tip of the pin at the intersection of the seam connecting the two triangles and their corresponding ¼″ seam allowances. Push it through and secure it. When you stitch the square to the pieced triangles, sew through the point you have marked with your pin. After stitching, look at your seam. Is the point of the triangle exactly ¼″ from what will be the outside edge of the block? If so, you can proceed.

Machines are different; fabric weights vary. If it seems that the top piece, when pinned, is constantly being urged over a bit by your presser foot, and you are just missing perfectly matched points, compensate by pinning just slightly beyond the tips of your triangles or by stitching just a bit to the right of your pin mark.

Save yourself as much work as you can. Units of blocks can be chain-pieced just as single pieces are. Sew the top right-hand square to the other two to complete the row. Sew the other two sets of three squares together to make three rows of three squares. Press seams well.

Lay out your three rows of blocks as you want to sew them. Sew the top row to the center row, pin-basting at seam intersections. As you sew more and more pieces together, all of your very small and somewhat inevitable inaccuracies will start to add up. It is critical that joints match. When one piece that must be sewn to another is larger than it should be, you can ease in the fullness: pin so the seams match; put the larger piece on the bottom, and pull on the top piece to stretch it gently as you sew. Your machine feed dogs will help you to ease in the fullness. One hundred percent cottons do this better than most synthetics will and this is one very good reason why most quilters prefer them.

Sew the third row onto the other two. Press your block flat. Your first block is finished!

Examine your work. Do all seams meet where they should? With a ¼″ seam allowance around the entire block, are your triangle points in danger of getting lost in a seam? If your block passes your inspection, keep stitching. The fun is just beginning.

A Note on Sewing Over Pins

Quilters and other sewers disagree here. Some say that it is fine to sew over your pins. They won't hurt your machine and will help your sewing. Others caution that sewing over pins can damage your machine, will dull your needle and definitely weakens your stitching. I try to remove them as I sew, just before they are about to pass under my needle. But sometimes a pin is doing a very critical job; the fabric can't be allowed to budge even the slightest bit. Then I leave in the pin, and sew over it. Sometimes, I am just too lazy to remove my pins as I sew. I keep spare machine needles on hand to replace them if they break.

Assemble all the blocks in this quilt in the same way as the Shoo-Fly—step by step, chain-sewing like pieces together where possible. To help you figure out which piece to sew in what order, I have drawn piecing diagrams for each block; these diagrams are given on pages 37–40. See *Diagram 15* for an explanation of how to follow each piecing diagram. I am sure that after you have sewn a few blocks you will know almost intuitively how a block should go together. Do sew the blocks in the suggested order, however. You will gradually gain competence and confidence, as the patterns get more complicated. Save Clay's Choice, Puss in the Corner and the Box quilt blocks to do last. They require one new technique, "setting-in," which is explained below.

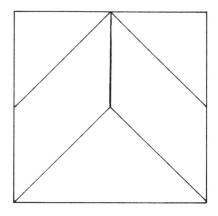

Diagram 16. *A unit of Puss in the Corner; note how the bottom triangle must be "set in" to the shape above it.*

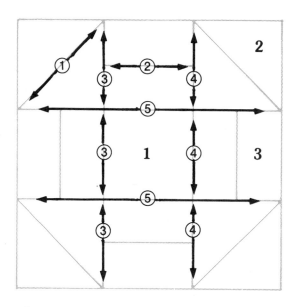

Diagram 15. *Numbers drawn on the piecing diagrams refer to the order in which each set of seams should be sewn. After the first (Shoo-Fly) block, the seams joining the* units *are not indicated, except where variations occur.*

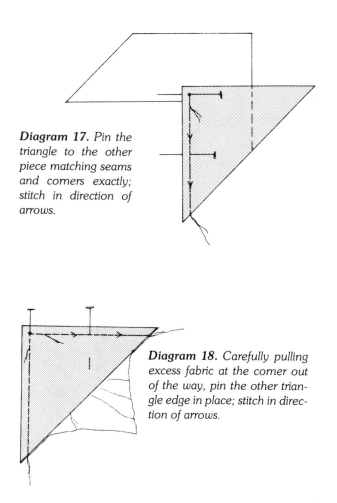

Diagram 17. *Pin the triangle to the other piece matching seams and corners exactly; stitch in direction of arrows.*

Diagram 18. *Carefully pulling excess fabric at the corner out of the way, pin the other triangle edge in place; stitch in direction of arrows.*

"SETTING-IN"

Setting one shape into another is really not difficult. Look at *Diagram 16* (a unit of Puss in the Corner); note how the base triangle must be "set" into the shape above it.

Put a pin through the exact intersection of the triangle's corner seam and that of the corner of the other shape as shown in *Diagram 17*. Begin by backstitching, then sew the seam from the point marked by your pin (and not beyond!) out to the edge of the triangle, following the directional arrows in the drawing. Next, carefully

pull the excess of the bottom piece out of the way of your triangle corner and pin the triangle edge to the corresponding side of the bottom shape; *Diagram 18*. Backstitching, sew the seam from the corner out to the edge. Press carefully so piece is flat.

The "setting-in" process will be used for three of the blocks in this quilt: Clay's Choice, Puss in the Corner and the Box.

CUTTING AND PIECING DIAGRAMS

1. SHOO-FLY

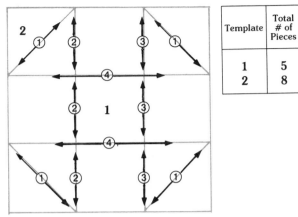

Template	Total # of Pieces	Plate
1	5	A
2	8	A

4. PRAIRIE QUEEN

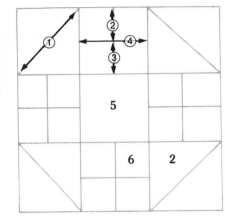

Template	Total # of Pieces	Plate
2	8	A
5	1	B
6	16	C

2. CHURN DASH

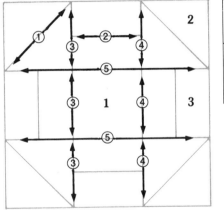

Template	Total # of Pieces	Plate
1	1	A
2	8	A
3	8	B

5. W.C.T.U.

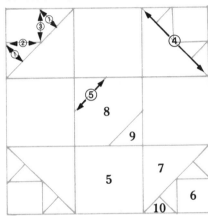

Template	Total # of Pieces	Plate
5	4	B
6	4	C
7	4	C
8	1	C
9	2	D
10	16	D

3. STAR

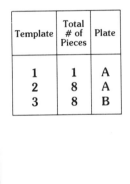

Template	Total # of Pieces	Plate
1	5	A
4	16	B

6. MOTHER'S DREAM

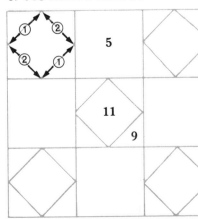

Template	Total # of Pieces	Plate
5	4	B
9	20	D
11	5	D

7. WHIRLWIND

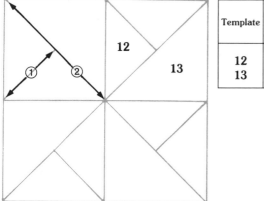

Template	Total # of Pieces	Plate
12	8	D
13	4	E

10. SAWTOOTH

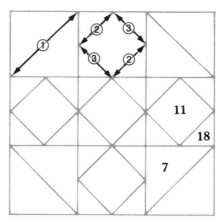

Template	Total # of Pieces	Plate
7	8	C
11	5	D
18	20	F

8. BEGGAR'S BLOCK

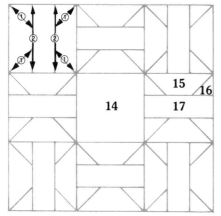

Template	Total # of Pieces	Plate
14	1	E
15	16	F
16	32	F
17	8	F

11. STEPPING STONES

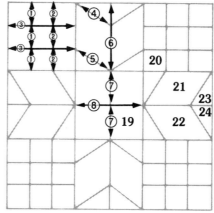

Template	Total # of Pieces	Plate
19	4	F
20	36	G
21	4	G
22	4	G
23	8	G
24	8	G

9. ROAD TO CALIFORNIA

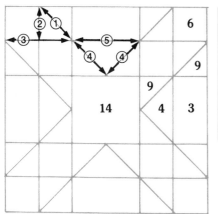

Template	Total # of Pieces	Plate
3	4	B
4	4	B
6	8	C
9	24	D
14	1	E

12. ROBBING PETER TO PAY PAUL

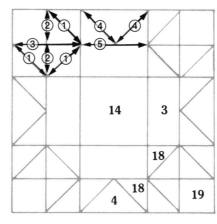

Template	Total # of Pieces	Plate
3	4	B
4	4	B
14	1	E
18	32	F
19	4	F

13. WEATHERVANE

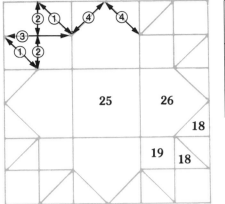

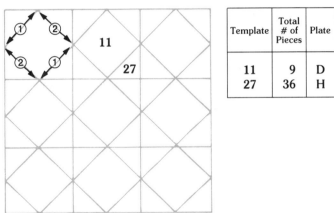

Template	Total # of Pieces	Plate
18	24	F
19	8	F
25	1	H
26	4	H

16. OLD TIPPECANOE

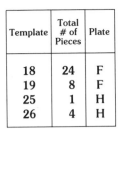

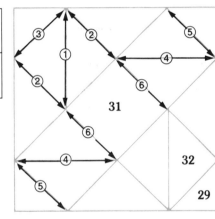

Template	Total # of Pieces	Plate
29	20	H
31	1	J
32	4	J

14. KANSAS STAR

Template	Total # of Pieces	Plate
11	9	D
27	36	H

17. NEXT DOOR NEIGHBOR

Template	Total # of Pieces	Plate
29	4	H
31	1	J
32	12	J

15. GRANDMOTHER'S FAVORITE

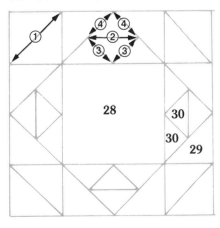

Template	Total # of Pieces	Plate
28	1	I
29	16	H
30	16	I

18. DOUBLE SQUARE

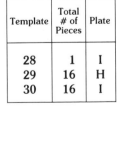

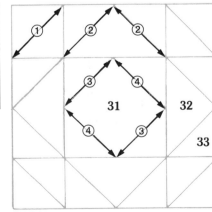

Template	Total # of Pieces	Plate
31	1	J
32	4	J
33	20	K

39

19. STAR PUZZLE

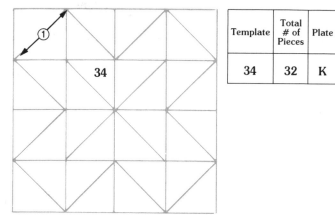

34

Template	Total # of Pieces	Plate
34	32	K

22. CLAY'S CHOICE

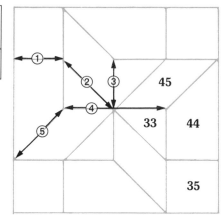

45

33

44

35

Template	Total # of Pieces	Plate
33	4	K
35	4	K
44	4	M
45	4	M

20. VIRGINIA REEL

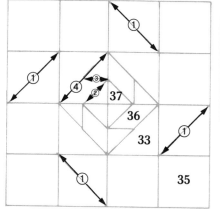

37

36

33

35

Template	Total # of Pieces	Plate
33	12	K
35	8	K
36	4	K
37	8	K

23. PUSS IN THE CORNER

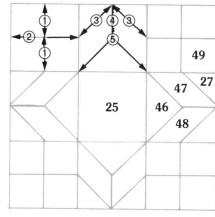

49

47

27

25

46

48

Template	Total # of Pieces	Plate
25	1	H
27	8	H
46	4	M
47	4	M
48	4	N
49	16	N

21. STAR AND CROSS

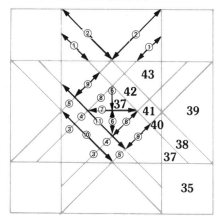

43

42

37

41

40

39

38

37

35

Template	Total # of Pieces	Plate
35	4	K
37	12	K
38	8	L
39	4	L
40	8	L
41	4	L
42	4	L
43	4	L
35		

24. BOX

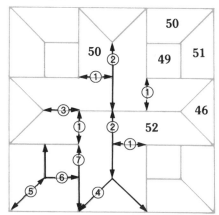

50

50

49

51

46

52

Template	Total # of Pieces	Plate
46	4	M
49	4	N
50	8	N
51	4	N
52	4	O

SASHING AND SET

Sashing, sash work and lattice are names for the strips of fabric that separate one block from another in a quilt. Not all quilts have sashing. The sashing in some quilts is very elaborate. This quilt has very simple sashing which is used to frame each block to set it off from the others. The final arrangement of your blocks, sashing and border is called the "set." The job you are about to do is called "setting together."

Look at the drawings on pages 6–7. Which one is the "set" for your quilt? Lay out your blocks following the diagram for your quilt's size. For instance, if you are making a double-sized quilt, you will lay out your blocks in a grid of four across and six down. Do this where you will be able to stand away from your arrangement to get an overall look at the entire "set."

Shift your blocks until you are satisfied with each one's position in relation to the rest. Try to distribute colors and dominant shapes. Think about where each block will be when your finished quilt is on your bed. Perhaps you have very favorite blocks that you would like to center in your set. You may have one block that never did come together to suit you. You could "hide" it under the pillow!

You are going to sew together your quilt blocks just as you sewed the units of each block. You will sew the blocks together into rows with short lengths of sashing between each block; then you will join the rows of blocks with sashing between each row. You probably won't be able to do this entire job in one session, so after deciding upon the final placement, pick up each row of blocks, keeping the far left block on top, and the rest of the blocks in that row in their proper order. With a piece of scrap paper and a pin, number and pin together the stack of blocks. Do this for each row, always keeping the far left block of each row on top. Then stack the rows of blocks in order by number, with Row 1 on top of the entire stack.

Pull out the fabric that you measured and set aside for your sashing at the very beginning. If you haven't cut the measured fabric into strips, do so now. Look at the drawing of your quilt's set. How many long and unpieced strips will you need to join your rows of blocks together? Cut these and put them aside. Check back to the drawing again. Four strips of the same fabric were measured and set aside to be used in your border. These may or may not be the same width as your sashing strips, depending upon the size of the quilt you are making. Cut these strips and set them aside.

Find the sashing template; check to be sure that it is the right one for your quilt size—the lengths are the same, but the widths vary. Trace and cut as many short sashes as you will need from the remaining sashing strips. If you are making a twin or double-sized quilt, you will need 18; a queen, 20; a king, 30.

Pin one of your short sashing strips to Block 1 of Row 1. The strip is exactly the length that your block should be. You may find that you have to ease or stretch the sides of some of your blocks as you sew in order to match the ends of the sash with the ends of your blocks. Be sure to pin through the ¼" seam allowance of the sash to any points on the block that must meet the seam. More than likely, not all of the edges of all your blocks are perfectly straight. By pinning the sashing on top of your block, you can use the very straight cut edge of the strip as a guide for your seam when you sew.

Pin and sew Block 2, Row 1 to your sewn sash. Sew a sash to Block 2, and continue in this pattern until you have completed the row; *Diagram 19*. Be sure to keep the row numbered with your pinned scrap of paper. Sew each row in this same way. Before joining the rows together, press your seams toward the sashing and away from the bulk of your blocks' seams.

Pick up the long strips of sashing that you have set aside. To prepare these strips for pinning and sewing, you must measure and mark where the strip must meet each intersection of sash and block. To do this, check

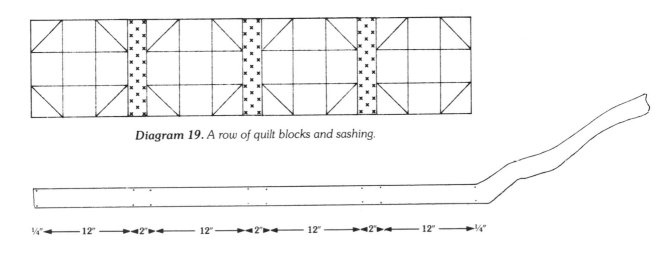

Diagram 19. A row of quilt blocks and sashing.

¼" ◄— 12" —►◄2"►◄ — 12" —►◄2"►◄ — 12" —►◄2"►◄ — 12" —►¼"

Diagram 20. This long sash has been marked for joining to a row of four quilt blocks.

back to the table listing the specifications for your quilt. Find out how wide your sashing is supposed to be when sewn. (Do not include the ¼″ seam allowances on either side.) Measure the widths of several of the sewn sashes between your blocks to check your number. The two should be the same. For a double-sized quilt, the sewn sash is 2 inches wide. Starting at one end of your long strip, measure and mark off your strip as shown in *Diagram 20*. Note that the measurement starts ¼″ from the edge of the sash for the seam allowance. The dots mark the exact point at which block-sash-block seams should intersect the sash.

Pin one marked sash to Row 1. Be sure to match ends, joints, and seams. Use your marks to pin the long sashing at the intersections of the stitched sashing accurately. Ease in any fullness wherever necessary. Continue to join your rows together with the sashing as you have done for Row 1. Press seams towards sashing.

A FRAME FOR YOUR QUILT—THE BORDER

The border of a quilt is its frame. It can be pieced in the same way blocks are pieced. Sometimes a very intricate border is used to contrast with a simple set of blocks. Not all quilts have a border. The quilt in this book has a very simple one. It is simple in two ways: it is very plain so that it will not compete with the many different blocks in the top and it is very easy to sew together.

Look back to the line drawing of your quilt. Your border is made up of three strips of fabric: a wide outside strip (the outer border), a narrow, contrasting middle strip (the middle border) and an inner border. These three strips are sewn together into one wide strip, which is then sewn to your quilt top.

You will need four outer border strips—two for the short sides and two for the long sides of your quilt. The lengths of each of these sets will vary according to the size of your quilt. Check the Table of Lengths and Widths on page 12 and find out how long yours must be. (If you have made adjustments to any of the sizes given in the table, be sure to keep those in mind, and make any other changes necessary at this point.) You may find that some of your narrow strips will have to be pieced so that they will be long enough to be sewn into your border; if you do piece them, be sure to press the seams flat.

Referring to the drawing of your quilt size (pages 6–7), sew each set of strips together in their proper order making four wide border strips—two "lengths" and two "widths." Do not pull on these strips as you sew them together; they are narrow and will stretch easily.

When you have sewn all of your strips together into four wide borders, press your seams flat. Be sure to press seams away from the edge along which you plan to quilt.

To be sure that the seams of your blocks and sashing intersect the seam of your border exactly where they

should, you must "tick off" or mark these intersections just as you did for your horizontal sashing. If you want your quilt top to lie flat, you must keep your border "on square" with the rest of your blocks. Pick up one of the borders that is to be sewn along the width of your top and lay it flat on your table. Lay out your quilt top where you can see it while you mark your border. Look at your quilt. Starting at one end of your border, and along the side that is to be sewn to the top, measure in the width of your border plus one inch, and mark the spot with a pencil tick or pin.

This is the exact point at which you will begin the seam when you sew your border to your top. Continue measuring down the length of your border, ticking off the 12″ for a block and the 1½ or 2 inches, depending on your quilt's size, for as many blocks and strips as you have across the width of your quilt. When you have ticked off the 12″ for the last block in the row, you will have marked the exact spot that your seam must end. Continue to measure along the length, adding the width of the border plus an inch. Mark or pin. Measure and mark your other three border strips in the same way along the edge that is to be sewn to your top.

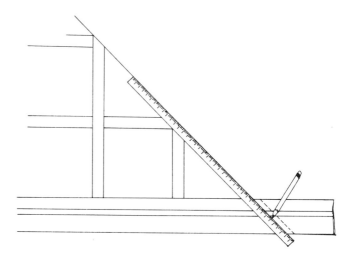

Diagram 21. Draw a light pencil line at a 45° angle across the border strip to mark the sewing line.

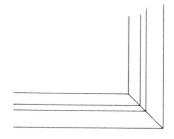

Diagram 22. A perfectly mitered border corner.

With right sides facing, pin one border strip to its corresponding edge of your quilt top. Be sure to match your pins or marks with all intersecting block and sashing seams. You are sure to find that at this point all of your little inaccuracies have added up. Don't worry: this happens to all of us. Some blocks may have to be stretched a bit, and others may need to be eased to fit between your measured marks. Make them fit within the grid you have measured. Do not be tempted to let them all "slide" down the seam "just a little."

Beginning in ¼″ from the edge of your corner block, stitch and backstitch, keeping the ¼″ at the edge of the block unsewn, and sew your border to your top. End and backstitch ¼″ from the edge of the opposite corner block (marked with a pin). Pin and sew the other three borders to their corresponding sides in the same way. Press all of your seams flat, pressing seams toward your border and away from the bulk of your seamed blocks.

To miter and join the corners of your border, lay one corner of your quilt out flat. Fold one edge of the quilt over to meet the other edge of the corner. Finger press the 45° angle and fold formed. Smooth the unsewn ends of the border flat, matching the two long edges. Carefully lay down your long metal ruler along the line formed by the fold of your top and over the width of your border. Carefully draw a light pencil line along the edge of your ruler to continue the line of the fold onto your border as shown in *Diagram 21*. This line is your *sewing line*, NOT your *cutting line*. Pin the borders together along this line, and cut away the excess, leaving a ½″ seam allowance beyond your pencilled line. Unpin. Then repin, this time carefully matching the intersection of the sewn strips as they meet your pencilled seam line. Sew the seam, beginning at the outside edge and stitching toward your quilt top center, backstitching at the beginning and end of your seam. Open up your mitered corner; see *Diagram 22*. If it suits you, press it flat. Then measure, butt, sew and press the other three corners.

Congratulations! Your quilt top is finished!

MARKING YOUR QUILT TOP

Antique quilts were very closely quilted for several reasons. For many quilters, this was the joy of the work. Piecing was a solitary task; but, quilting . . . that was different. Friends would get together, put up a quilt in a frame and stitch and gossip. It was a grand time for socializing and catching up on the news. A woman took pride in her small, even stitches. A very special quilt would show off this expertise. But old quilts were also heavily quilted for a very practical reason. They were generally filled with cotton batting. This was not "all of a piece" like our modern version. Close stitches were used to anchor the wads of cotton in place, and to keep them from shifting with use and laundering.

When using the polyester batting that is available today, it is not necessary to quilt a top as closely as in the past. However, too little quilting can put stress on those stitches that you do make. As a general guideline, do not leave more than a six-by-six-square-inch section unquilted.

You now have to decide how much quilting you want to do. Lay out your top and look at it. The individual blocks can be outline-quilted along seam lines. The sashing is not too wide; it can be outline-quilted as well. But what about the borders? What do you want to do here? The outer border strip will need more than just outline quilting both for aesthetic and practical reasons.

There are lots of possibilities for quilting in this strip. Look at the five photographs of the sampler quilts to find out how five different quilters solved the problem. If yours is a solid fabric, a distinct pattern traced from a commercial or homemade cardboard template might work well. See page 47 for a selection of filler patterns that might work well on your border. Teacups and saucers are very traditional "templates" for circular patterns. You may want to measure and mark out a series of lines perpendicular to the seam of the outer border strip to quilt (see the quilt on the front cover of this book). If you choose to do any of these, be sure to do some measuring and figuring on paper before you begin marking on your top. You want to be sure that any motif will be equally spaced along all of the edges of your quilt, and that the lines come together in a pleasing way at the corners of your top. One way to do this is to pick a motif that is as wide as a number that will divide evenly (with no remainder) into the length and width of your top. Another is to start by measuring and tracing at the center of each border, working out from the center toward the corner. You may have to do a little "fudging" in your spacing toward the corners to get them to work well.

The easiest pattern to mark onto this wide strip is a series of parallel lines, measured out from the seam toward the quilt's edge. When quilted, these lines will divide the wide strip into several narrow channels. If this is your choice, with a light pencil line, draw in two or three parallel lines in this wide strip. Take care that these lines intersect at each of the mitered corners of your top.

ASSEMBLING YOUR QUILT

Making the Back

Traditionally, not much attention was paid to the back of a quilt. The pioneer woman who was hoarding every scrap of fabric, using it and reusing it in piecework did not have the luxury of a solid piece of fabric to use as a back for her quilt. Sometimes the back of a very old quilt is made of as many pieces as are in the front. As fabric became more plentiful, the usual back for a quilt was unbleached muslin. This may still have been made of several pieces that were seamed together.

You will also have to sew several lengths of fabric together to have one piece large enough to back your quilt. *Do not be tempted to use a bedsheet.* Although conveniently just the right size, a sheet is too closely woven to make it easy to quilt. Measure the exact dimensions of your quilt top. Keeping in mind that most fabric is 45″ wide, minus an inch or so for cutting away selvages and shrinkage, figure the best way to piece two or more lengths of fabric to make one piece at least an inch larger (two or three is even better) than your quilt's dimensions on all four sides. Remember to add several inches to the length as well as the width to allow for shrinkage. In general, a twin or double quilt requires slightly more than two times the length of the top (allowing 4 to 6 inches for shrinkage); a queen, or king, slightly more than three times the length.

Since you will probably have to buy the fabric for your back, you will be able to give it more consideration than your colonial counterpart. Some people prefer the unbleached muslin back because it is very traditional. Often this is only 36 inches wide, so you may have to do a little refiguring if you decide to use it. Others like a solid back because the wonderful designs made by their quilting stitches can be enjoyed on the back as well as the front. Some choose to use a coordinating print as a back for decorative reasons. A back that is carefully pieced makes a quilt that is acceptably reversible.

Before you piece the back for your quilt, be sure that you have clipped selvages and have pre-shrunk and pressed your fabric. If you are piecing two lengths together, join them along a center seam; if you are piecing three lengths together, join two lengths to a center panel. Press your seams flat, to one side.

While you have your quilt dimensions in hand, and are shopping for a quilt back, you should also purchase your batt.

Batting

Batting is the filling that is sewn into your quilt between the top and the back. Be sure to buy a batt that is somewhat larger than your quilt. If you cannot find a batt that is large enough for your quilt, you will have to piece it. (Try to avoid this, if you can.)

If it is necessary to piece your batt, use one of these two methods:

(1) **To hand-piece:** butt the edges to be joined together, then handstitch with long and overlapping cross-stitches.
(2) **To machine-piece:** *slightly* overlap the batting edges to be joined, then join with a long zigzag stitch.

There are basically three kinds of batting that are readily available. One is a *needle-punched* polyester batt: it is soft and fluffy. It has the "hand" of an old cotton batt. Another is a *bonded* polyester batt: it has a glazed surface which looks as if a hot iron had been held over the fluff to "melt" it slightly. The third is a cotton/poly-

ester batt. Cotton and wool batts exist, but are not very common. Each type of batting has advantages and drawbacks. The needle-punched batt is very soft and easy to stitch. However, since it has not been "bonded," the polyester fibers, especially when used with a top of cotton/polyester blends, tend to migrate through the quilt top, causing what is known as "bearding." This tendency is particularly noticeable on dark fabrics. The bonded batt prevents most of this migration, but not all. It has a "plastic" feel to it that some find undesirable. The cotton/polyester batt is new. It is thin, and may be the most like the traditional quilt filler. It does shrink—so be sure to wash it first before using it in your quilt.

If it seems that I feel there is no perfect solution to the choice of a quilt batt, you are right. My advice is to start by using the bonded batt for this quilt. As you gain experience, you may want to experiment with the others. They do have something to offer to a quilter. You will soon be able to make your own choices about which will work best in a given situation.

Not "Bacon-Lettuce-and-Tomato," But . . .

You are about to turn your quilt top, batt and back into a "textile sandwich." I do this job on a bare floor so that I can lay the whole quilt out at one time, and can be very sure that all the layers are smooth and "on center."

Press your back. Lay it on the floor, right side down, seam side up. I line up the center seam of my back along the edge of one floorboard to be sure that it stays straight. Use masking tape to fasten the back to the floor, keeping it very smooth and wrinkle-free.

Carefully open your batt and center it over your quilt back. Four hands can make this job easier, if extras are available. Smooth the batt evenly over your back. Work any ridges and wrinkles out from the center toward the edges.

Press your quilt top. This is the last chance you will get to put an iron to it, so do it the very best that you can.

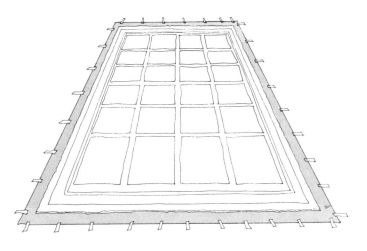

Diagram 23. A "textile sandwich": quilt top, batting and quilt back (taped to the floor).

Lay your pressed top, right side up, over the batting. Line up the center of the top with the center seam of your back. (If your back has no center seam, devise some other guide to help you center your top over your back.) Smooth the top over the batting, working from the center toward the edges. Be sure that some back and batting extend beyond the top on all four sides of your quilt; see *Diagram 23.*

With a long, strong needle and thread, baste the three layers of your quilt together without lifting the quilt from the floor. Use a light-colored thread; a dark color can leave behind a shadow when the basting is removed. Use long running stitches. Work from the center toward the edges. Do one quadrant at a time, basting in rows of stitches as shown in *Diagram 24.* Space your rows three to four inches apart. Baste well. Your quilt may be pushed in and out of a hoop many times before it is finished. Use a thimble to help you push the needle through all the thicknesses of your quilt. The basting must go through all three layers. Instead of tying a knot to end your thread, simply backstitch and let the end hang freely. It will be easy to find when you are ready to remove the basting.

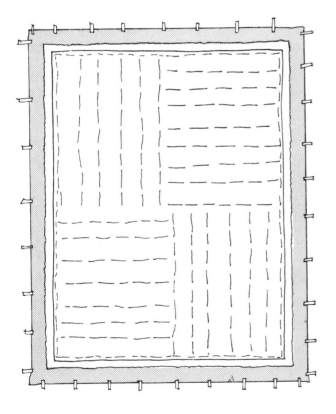

Diagram 24. A quilt basted in quadrants.

When your quilt is completely basted (edges too), pull up your tape, securing the back to the floor. You can trim away any excess batting and back—but leave at least an inch or more of each as a safety margin around all four sides.

QUILTING YOUR QUILT

Quilting serves a very practical purpose: the small, evenly spaced stitches hold the three layers of your quilt together and keep its filling from shifting out of place. Quilting is also decorative. A quilted surface is not flat; it has depth and texture. Quilting stitches can emphasize parts of your pieced design or can superimpose a totally new pattern over it.

The technique of quilting is a very simple one. The quilting stitch is a small, even running stitch. Old-time quilters stitched twelve or more to an inch. Few contemporary quilters can match that. But fabrics and fillers have changed. Concentrate on making your stitches even; small ones will come with practice. To begin quilting, center a block in your hoop. It is usually best to quilt from the center blocks out toward the border. Pull the surface of the quilt taut, smoothing any fullness out toward the edges of the hoop. Screw your hoop tight to hold the stretched block in place. Choose a needle.

Quilting needles are called "betweens." They are short and sharp. Shorter needles make shorter stitches. If a #8 or a #10 seems just too small for your fingers, use one that is slightly longer. Try to work your way to a smaller needle as you gain experience in quilting. Use cotton-covered quilting thread or 100% cotton thread coated with a little beeswax.

In a multi-colored quilt, it can be hard to choose a quilting thread color. Unless you are an expert quilter, or have a specific reason to do otherwise, choose one color that will blend into those in your top. For light-colored combinations, off-white thread works well. Using a contrasting color to quilt a solid background can be very effective—but be sure your stitches can stand up to the scrutiny such a contrast will invite!

Thread your needle with the end of the thread coming off the spool. Cut your thread about 18" long, and knot the cut end with a small single knot. Put your thimble on the middle finger of your sewing hand. Don't protest . . . instead, persist. If you have never used a thimble, learn to use one now. Otherwise, your poor finger will suffer some real and painful abuse. You will never be able to quilt very long at one time, will not find the work relaxing and, in the end, will look for ways to avoid working on your quilt. Find a thimble that fits—and use it.

Your sampler quilt is outline-quilted. This is a technique that involves stitching around pieced shapes that you want to emphasize. By quilting along the side of the seam without the seam allowance, you will be able to make small and even stitches. Avoid sewing through seam allowances wherever possible: it makes quilting hard work, and hard work is tough to do well. Pick a spot to start. Put your needle through your quilt from the underside, coming up through your top at the point where you want to begin stitching. Tug slightly on your thread to pull your knot through the back to bury it in your batting. Begin stitching a fine running stitch. Keep one hand under your hoop to feel for the tip of your needle as you sew through all three layers. With practice, this becomes an in-out rock-and-roll motion. You may find it easiest to make several stitches on your needle at a time. Quilting becomes a rhythmic activity with practice. You will enjoy it as your motion becomes sure and your stitches easy. To end stitching, tie a small knot in your thread close to your quilt's surface and take one more stitch, pulling the needle up to the surface about an inch from your last stitch and burying your knot securely in your batt.

FINISHING TOUCHES

There are lots of good reasons for making your own binding to finish the edge of your quilt. The quality of purchased binding probably won't measure up to the other fabrics in your quilt; it is very narrow and it is expensive. Also, the colors available may not match or coordinate well with your quilt. Make your own. It is easy. It lasts. It is good-looking.

Here is how to do it. Since your quilt has no curved edges, you don't have to make bias binding. You have already measured out or set aside the fabric for this job. Pull out the piece you have saved for the binding and press it flat. Cut your fabric into strips two inches wide and as long as your piece will allow. Refer back to your chart to find out the total length needed to bind your quilt. Allow a little extra. Sew your strips into one very long strip. Press your seams to one side. Folding the width of your strip in half as you press, iron in a fold along the entire length of your strip. Make a double fold along one long edge of the strip, folding and pressing the raw edge in to meet the center fold.

Trim away the excess back and batting from your quilt, leaving a ¼" margin of both around all four sides. Machine stitch your binding to your quilt with a ½" seam allowance, sewing the unfolded edge of the strip to the top of your quilt with right sides facing. Miter (requires a little practice and pre-pinning) or ease your binding around corners. Handstitch the folded edge of your binding to the back of your quilt with a small overcast stitch.

ONE LAST, BUT VERY IMPORTANT, DETAIL

Old quilts have given many of us lots of joy. Each is a statement of some sort made by its maker. Some quilts mark special events in a quilter's life. How much more we can enjoy sharing it when we can put a name to the hand that stitched that event into history. Do sign your quilt. Be sure to date it. If you are not a whiz with embroidery thread, sign it carefully with indelible ink—on the front, if you are brave; on the back, if you are not. If you can't face writing on your quilt at all, make a label (you can practice on several to get it just the way you want it) and then sew the label to your quilt. Share your accomplishment with someone else: sign your quilt.

CARING FOR YOUR QUILT

If your quilt is well quilted, you should be able to machine wash (on the gentle cycle) and dry it. If you lack the nerve to test your stitches, it can be washed by hand in a bathtub. Be sure to rinse it many times to remove all of the soap, and squeeze the excess water from it very gently. Lay it out flat to dry. Never hang a wet quilt from one line—nobody's stitches can hold up to that kind of abuse. If you must hang it from a line, lay your quilt over several lines to dry.

Dry-cleaning can actually shorten the life of a quilt. Don't do it unless your fabrics demand that sort of care. Never, ever, ever iron a quilt.

If you have to pack your quilt away for a time, fold it lightly in tissue paper. Never store it in plastic. And take it out to refold it from time to time.

Filling Patterns

Metric Conversion Chart

CONVERTING INCHES TO CENTIMETERS AND YARDS TO METERS

mm — millimeters   cm — centimeters   m — meters

INCHES INTO MILLIMETERS AND CENTIMETERS
(Slightly rounded off for convenience)

inches	mm		cm	inches	cm	inches	cm	inches	cm
⅛	3mm			5	12.5	21	53.5	38	96.5
¼	6mm			5½	14	22	56	39	99
⅜	10mm	or	1cm	6	15	23	58.5	40	101.5
½	13mm	or	1.3cm	7	18	24	61	41	104
⅝	15mm	or	1.5cm	8	20.5	25	63.5	42	106.5
¾	20mm	or	2cm	9	23	26	66	43	109
⅞	22mm	or	2.2cm	10	25.5	27	68.5	44	112
1	25mm	or	2.5cm	11	28	28	71	45	114.5
1¼	32mm	or	3.2cm	12	30.5	29	73.5	46	117
1½	38mm	or	3.8cm	13	33	30	76	47	119.5
1¾	45mm	or	4.5cm	14	35.5	31	79	48	122
2	50mm	or	5cm	15	38	32	81.5	49	124.5
2½	65mm	or	6.5cm	16	40.5	33	84	50	127
3	75mm	or	7.5cm	17	43	34	86.5		
3½	90mm	or	9cm	18	46	35	89		
4	100mm	or	10cm	19	48.5	36	91.5		
4½	115mm	or	11.5cm	20	51	37	94		

YARDS TO METERS
(Slightly rounded off for convenience)

yards	meters	yards	meters	yards	meters	yards	meters	yards	meters
⅛	0.15	2⅛	1.95	4⅛	3.80	6⅛	5.60	8⅛	7.45
¼	0.25	2¼	2.10	4¼	3.90	6¼	5.75	8¼	7.55
⅜	0.35	2⅜	2.20	4⅜	4.00	6⅜	5.85	8⅜	7.70
½	0.50	2½	2.30	4½	4.15	6½	5.95	8½	7.80
⅝	0.60	2⅝	2.40	4⅝	4.25	6⅝	6.10	8⅝	7.90
¾	0.70	2¾	2.55	4¾	4.35	6¾	6.20	8¾	8.00
⅞	0.80	2⅞	2.65	4⅞	4.50	6⅞	6.30	8⅞	8.15
1	0.95	3	2.75	5	4.60	7	6.40	9	8.25
1⅛	1.05	3⅛	2.90	5⅛	4.70	7⅛	6.55	9⅛	8.35
1¼	1.15	3¼	3.00	5¼	4.80	7¼	6.65	9¼	8.50
1⅜	1.30	3⅜	3.10	5⅜	4.95	7⅜	6.75	9⅜	8.60
1½	1.40	3½	3.20	5½	5.05	7½	6.90	9½	8.70
1⅝	1.50	3⅝	3.35	5⅝	5.15	7⅝	7.00	9⅝	8.80
1¾	1.60	3¾	3.45	5¾	5.30	7¾	7.10	9¾	8.95
1⅞	1.75	3⅞	3.55	5⅞	5.40	7⅞	7.20	9⅞	9.05
2	1.85	4	3.70	6	5.50	8	7.35	10	9.15

AVAILABLE FABRIC WIDTHS

25″	65cm	50″	127cm
27″	70cm.	54″/56″	140cm
35″/36″	90cm	58″/60″	150cm
39″	100cm	68″/70″	175cm
44″/45″	115cm	72″	180cm
48″	122cm		

AVAILABLE ZIPPER LENGTHS

4″	10cm	10″	25cm	22″	55cm
5″	12cm	12″	30cm	24″	60cm
6″	15cm	14″	35cm	26″	65cm
7″	18cm	16″	40cm	28″	70cm
8″	20cm	18″	45cm	30″	75cm
9″	22cm	20″	50cm		

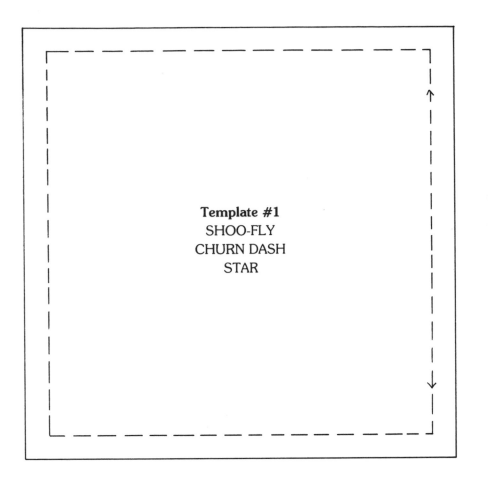

Template #1
SHOO-FLY
CHURN DASH
STAR

NOTE

Some of the templates in this section have been duplicated for your convenience. If you are making very durable templates that will stand up to repeated usage, you needn't make duplicates. When preparing the templates, check the sizes to avoid repeating the same shape; be sure to mark the template with the additional numbers and quilt block names to prevent confusion.

Template #2
SHOO-FLY
CHURN DASH
PRAIRIE QUEEN

PLATE A

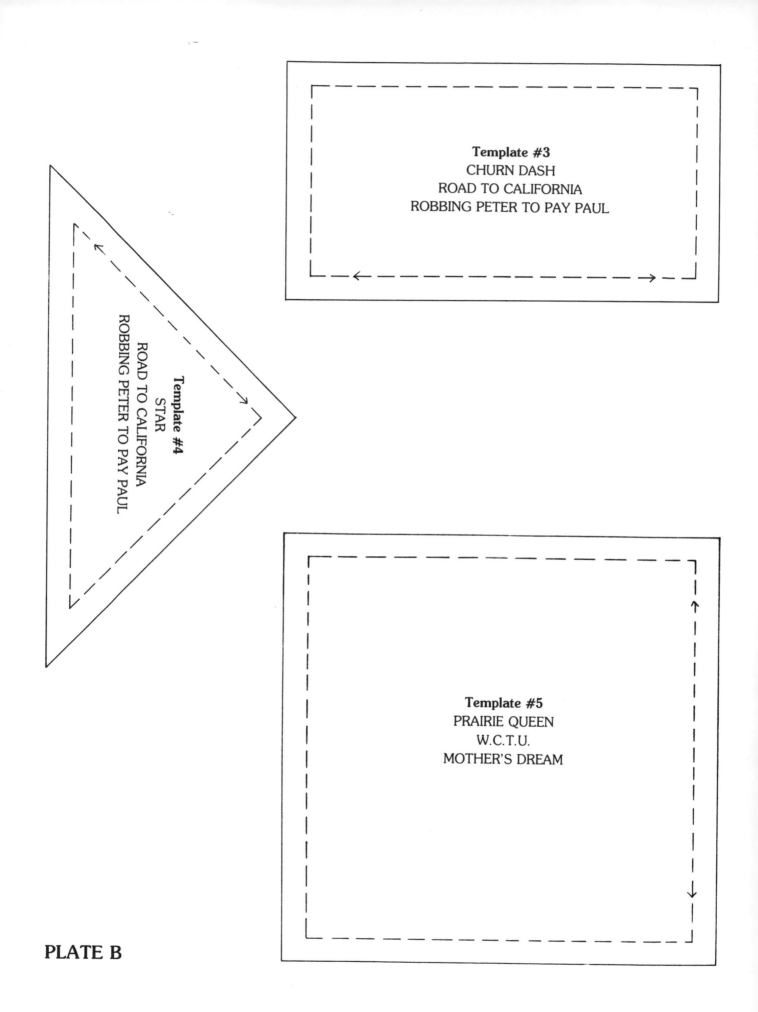

Template #3
CHURN DASH
ROAD TO CALIFORNIA
ROBBING PETER TO PAY PAUL

Template #4
STAR
ROAD TO CALIFORNIA
ROBBING PETER TO PAY PAUL

Template #5
PRAIRIE QUEEN
W.C.T.U.
MOTHER'S DREAM

PLATE B

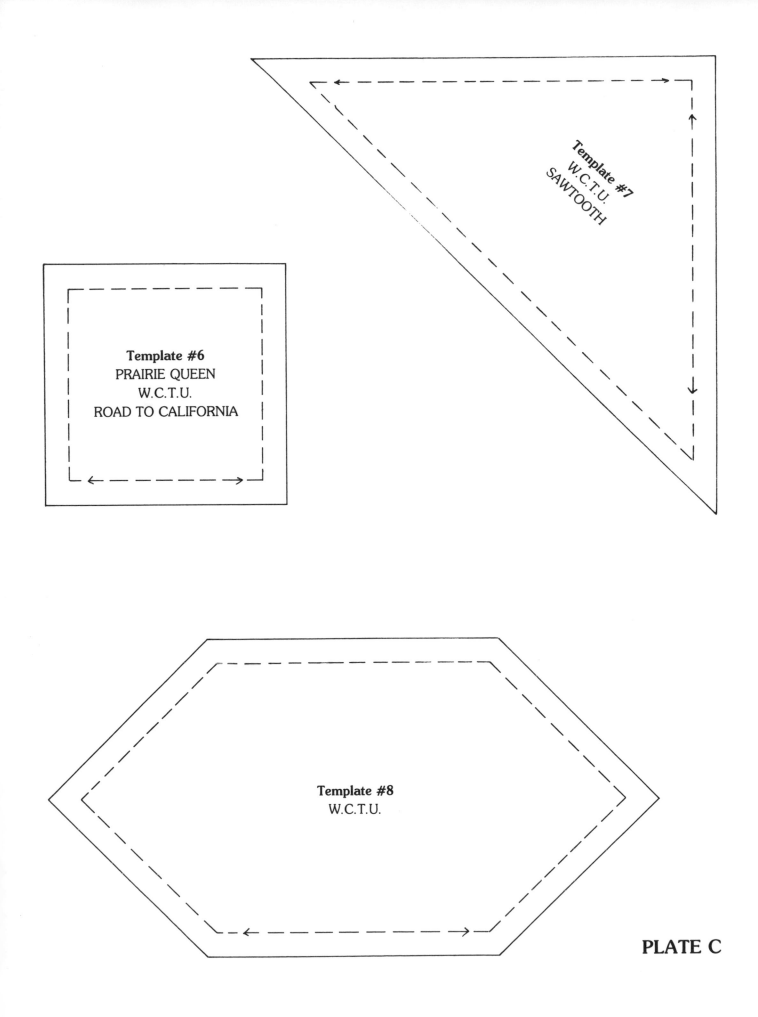

Template #6
PRAIRIE QUEEN
W.C.T.U.
ROAD TO CALIFORNIA

Template #7
W.C.T.U.
SAWTOOTH

Template #8
W.C.T.U.

PLATE C

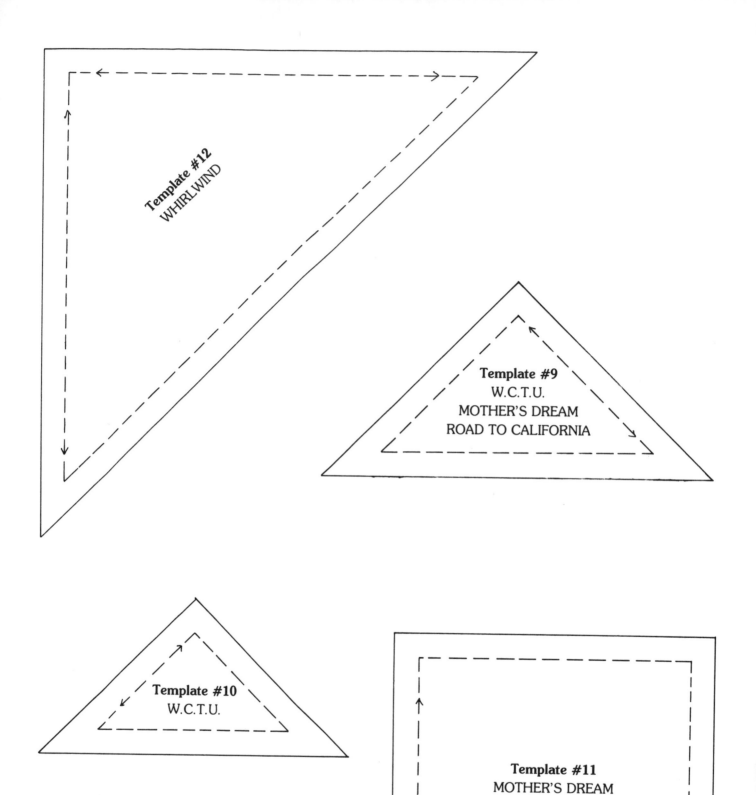

Template #12
WHIRLWIND

Template #9
W.C.T.U.
MOTHER'S DREAM
ROAD TO CALIFORNIA

Template #10
W.C.T.U.

Template #11
MOTHER'S DREAM
SAWTOOTH
KANSAS STAR

PLATE D

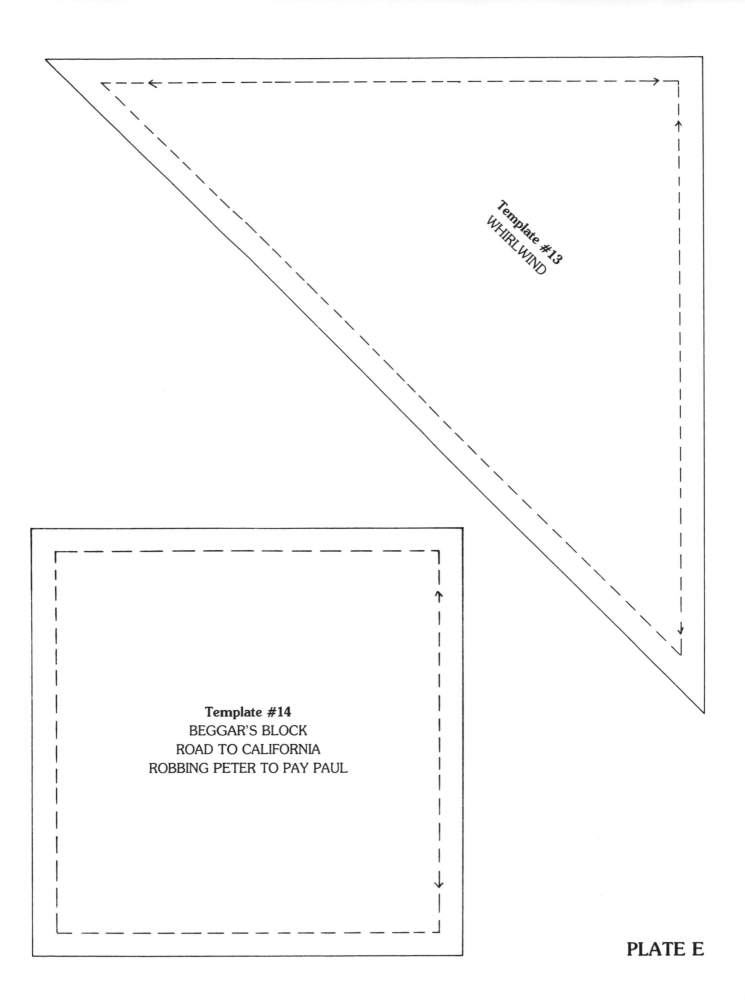

Template #13
WHIRLWIND

Template #14
BEGGAR'S BLOCK
ROAD TO CALIFORNIA
ROBBING PETER TO PAY PAUL

PLATE E

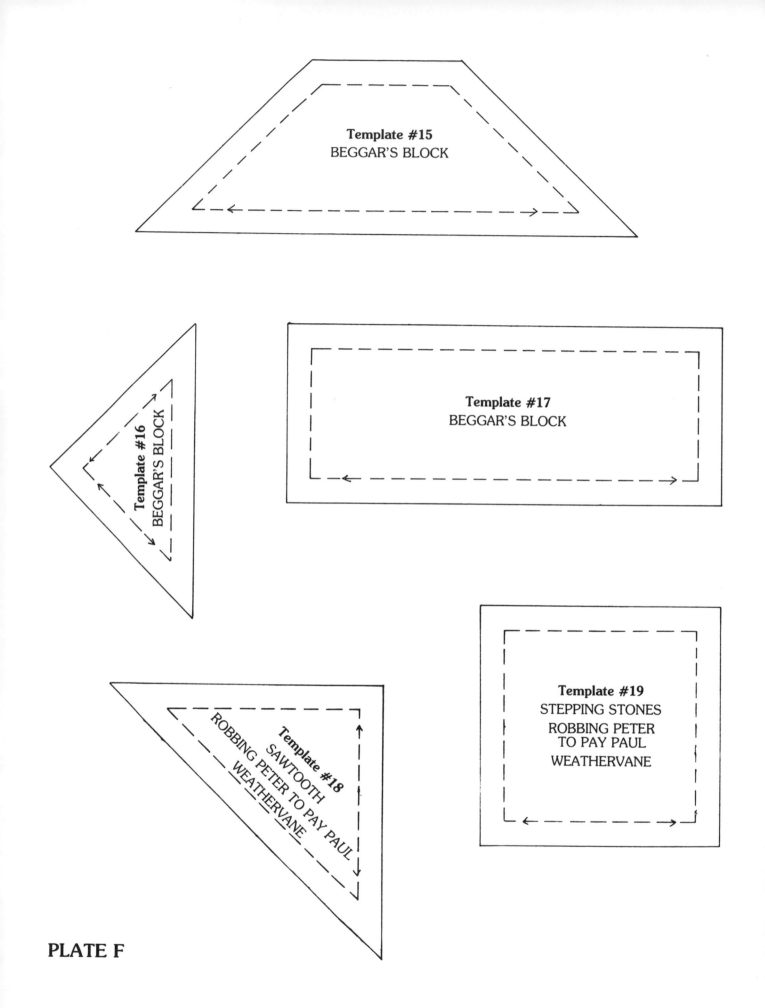

Template #15
BEGGAR'S BLOCK

Template #16
BEGGAR'S BLOCK

Template #17
BEGGAR'S BLOCK

Template #18
SAWTOOTH
ROBBING PETER TO PAY PAUL
WEATHERVANE

Template #19
STEPPING STONES
ROBBING PETER
TO PAY PAUL
WEATHERVANE

PLATE F

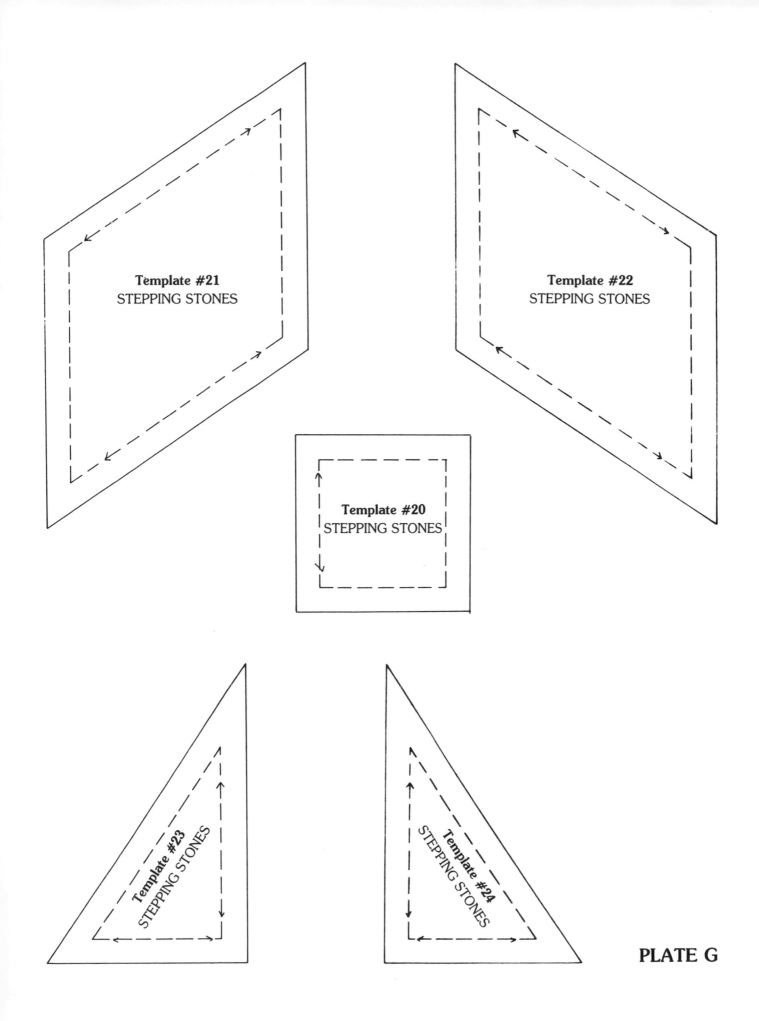

Template #21
STEPPING STONES

Template #22
STEPPING STONES

Template #20
STEPPING STONES

Template #23
STEPPING STONES

Template #24
STEPPING STONES

PLATE G

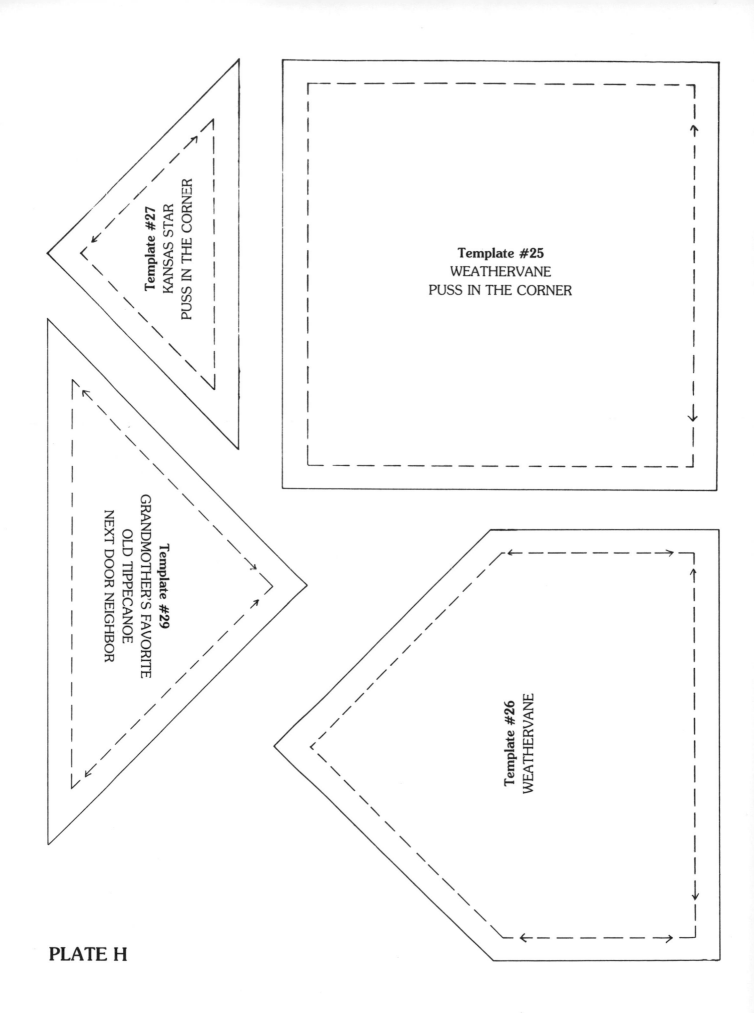

Template #27
KANSAS STAR
PUSS IN THE CORNER

Template #25
WEATHERVANE
PUSS IN THE CORNER

Template #29
GRANDMOTHER'S FAVORITE
OLD TIPPECANOE
NEXT DOOR NEIGHBOR

Template #26
WEATHERVANE

PLATE H

Template #28
GRANDMOTHER'S FAVORITE

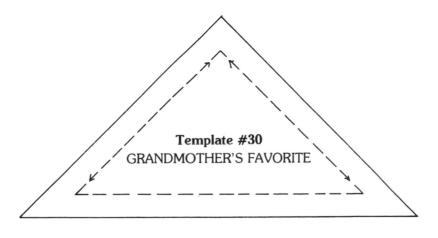

Template #30
GRANDMOTHER'S FAVORITE

PLATE I

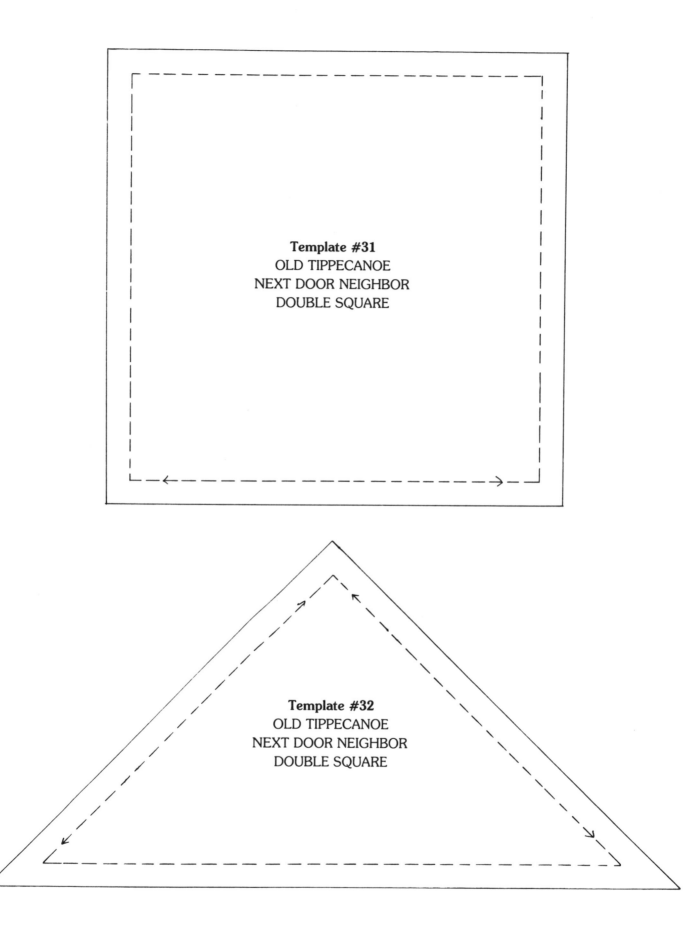

Template #31
OLD TIPPECANOE
NEXT DOOR NEIGHBOR
DOUBLE SQUARE

Template #32
OLD TIPPECANOE
NEXT DOOR NEIGHBOR
DOUBLE SQUARE

PLATE J

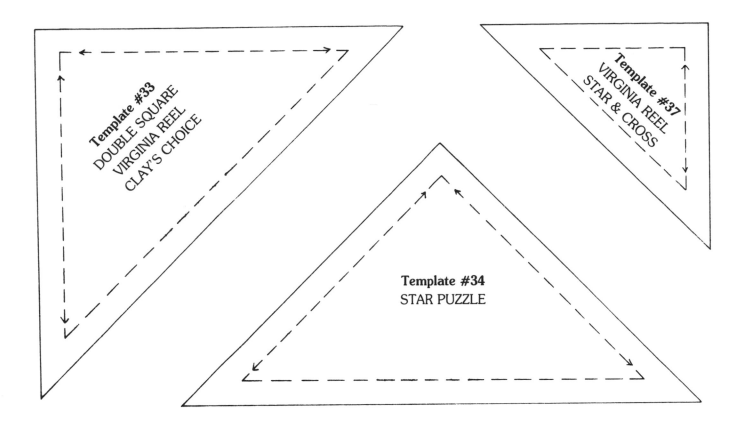

Template #33
DOUBLE SQUARE
VIRGINIA REEL
CLAY'S CHOICE

Template #37
VIRGINIA REEL
STAR & CROSS

Template #34
STAR PUZZLE

Template #35
VIRGINIA REEL
STAR & CROSS
CLAY'S CHOICE

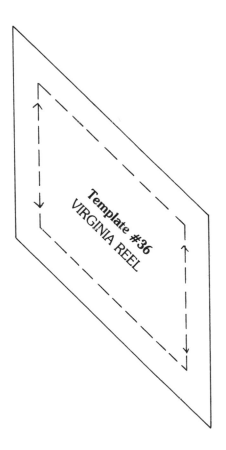

Template #36
VIRGINIA REEL

PLATE K

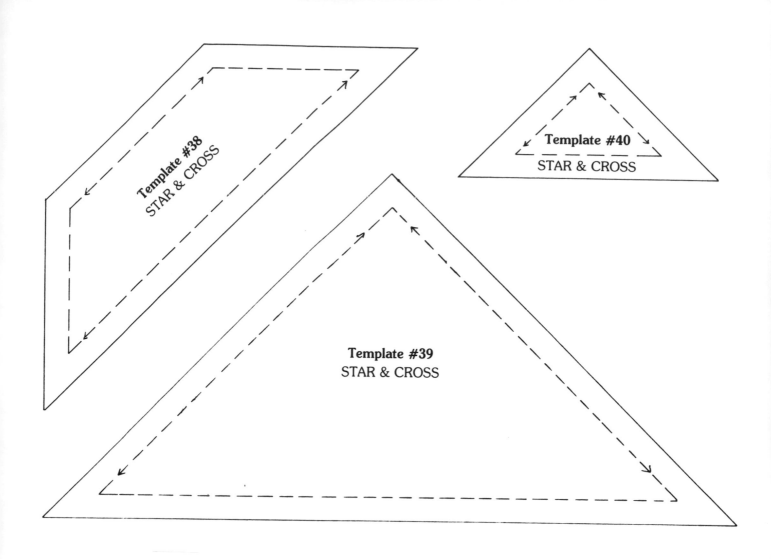

Template #38
STAR & CROSS

Template #40
STAR & CROSS

Template #39
STAR & CROSS

Template #41
STAR & CROSS

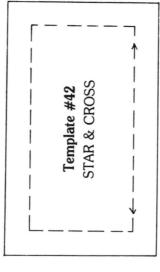

Template #42
STAR & CROSS

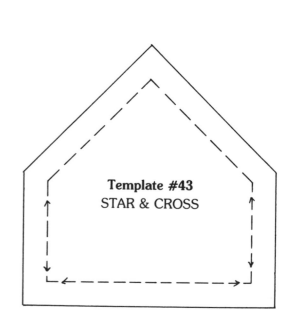

Template #43
STAR & CROSS

PLATE L

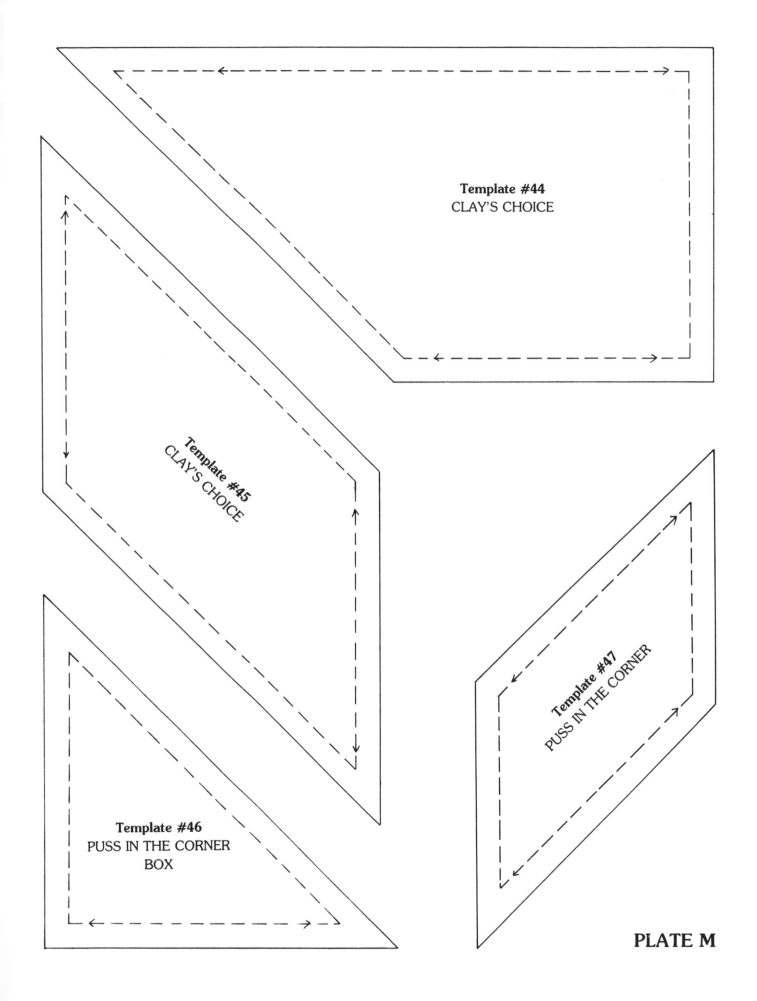

Template #44
CLAY'S CHOICE

Template #45
CLAY'S CHOICE

Template #46
PUSS IN THE CORNER
BOX

Template #47
PUSS IN THE CORNER

PLATE M

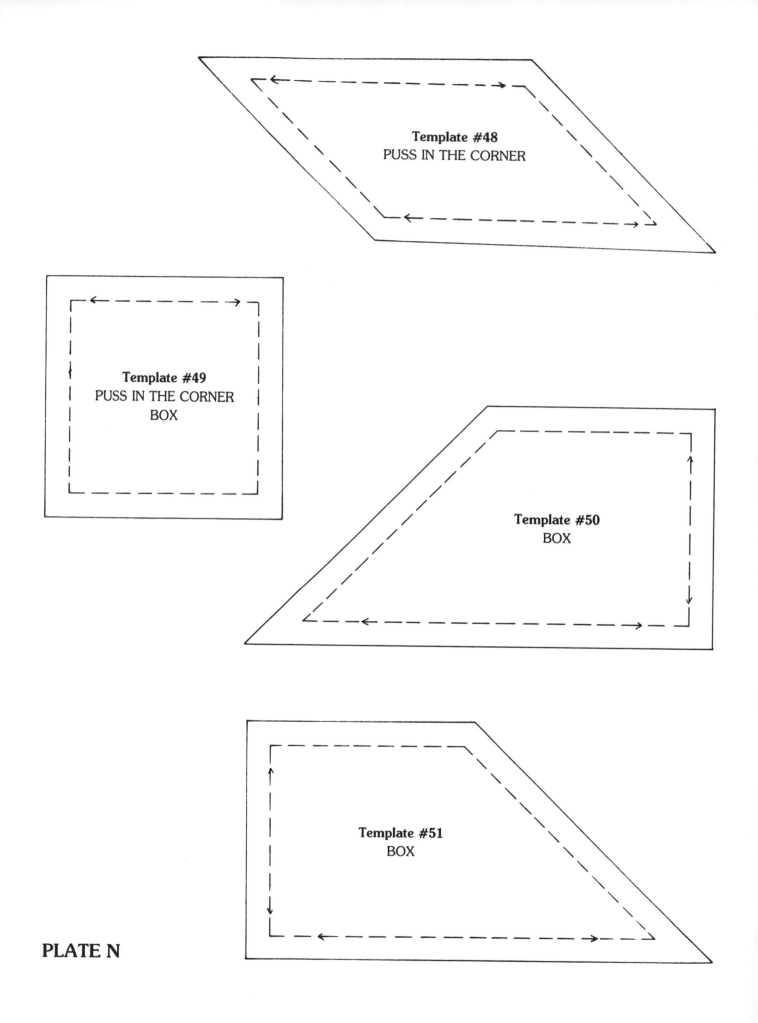

Template #48
PUSS IN THE CORNER

Template #49
PUSS IN THE CORNER
BOX

Template #50
BOX

Template #51
BOX

PLATE N

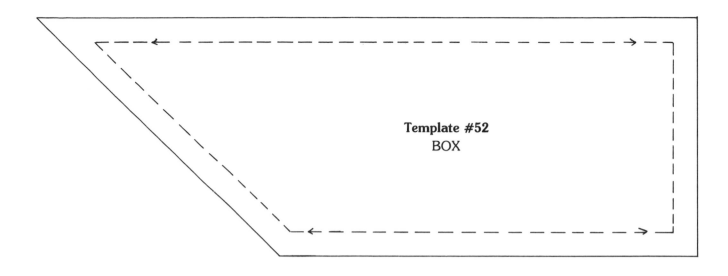

Template #52
BOX

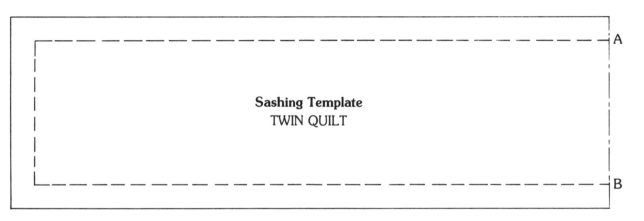

Sashing Template
TWIN QUILT

A

B

Tape templates together, matching dot/dash lines.

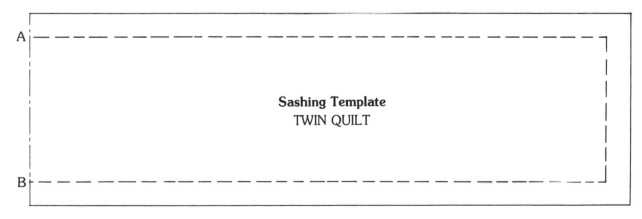

A

Sashing Template
TWIN QUILT

B

PLATE O

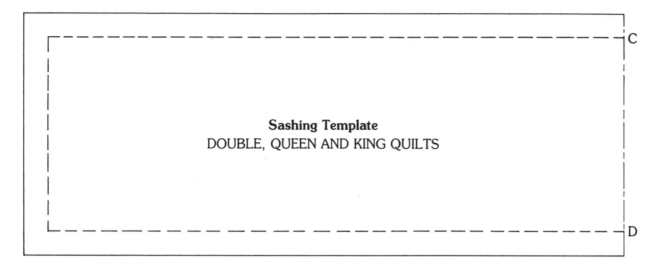

Sashing Template
DOUBLE, QUEEN AND KING QUILTS

C

D

Tape templates together, matching dot/dash lines.

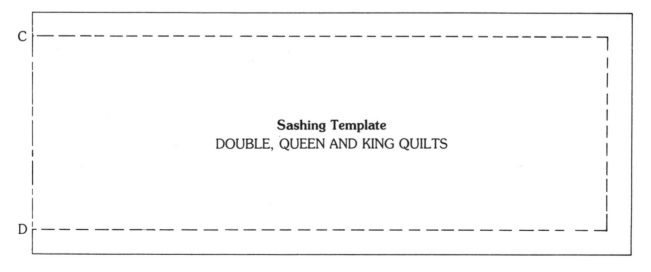

C

Sashing Template
DOUBLE, QUEEN AND KING QUILTS

D

PLATE P